Harness It

Harness It

Renewable Energy Technologies and Project Development Models Transforming the Grid

Michael Ginsberg

With Forewords by three of the greatest minds in renewable energy

Dr. Jeffrey D. Sachs, Dr. Arthur J. Nozik, and Dr. Vasilis M. Fthenakis

BEP BUSINESS EXPERT PRESS

First published in 2019 by
Business Expert Press, LLC
222 East 46th Street, New York, NY 10017
www.businessexpertpress.com

ISBN-13: 978-1-63157-931-8 (paperback)
ISBN-13: 978-1-63157-932-5 (e-book)

Business Expert Press Industry Profiles Collection

Collection ISSN: 2331-0065 (print)
Collection ISSN: 2331-0073 (electronic)

Cover and interior design by Exeter Premedia Services Private Ltd., Chennai, India

First edition: 2019

10 9 8 7 6 5 4 3 2 1

Printed in the United States of America.

To Jeffrey Hanley, for believing in me.

Abstract

Executive Summary: Following an overview of the technical and historical development of the electrical grid in the U.S. and Europe, this guide reviews hydropower, solar photovoltaics, wind energy, fuel cell, and battery technologies. Next, it presents models for the connection of these renewable energy sources from large-scale to on-site and community power/microgrids. The models are explained through case studies in the developed and developing worlds that explore how technical evaluations are conducted, policy incentives implemented, and project finance applied. Considering the increasing importance of renewable energy for climate change mitigation, this book provides an overview of how renewable energy sources are integrated into the grid to promote better understanding among students and business professionals in the utility sector and across industries.

Primary Audience: MBA and engineering students, and current business professionals managing a portfolio of energy investments (both clean technology and conventional fuels). Most literature on grid interconnection is highly technical, assuming an in-depth understanding of electrical engineering. With the rise of clean technologies and the diversity of interconnection models, this guide fills a gap in the existing literature by equipping non-technical business managers with the salient information they need to make critical decisions for their organizations.

Keywords

Renewable energy; grid integration; solar energy; sustainability; climate change; resiliency; wind energy; hydropower; green energy; solar photovoltaic; grid modernization; green technology; energy sources; energy economics

Contents

Endorsements

Ginsberg gives us a roadmap to making the electrification of everything sustainable and reliable, confronting what it takes to translate green visions into commercial reality.

> —**Carlos Pascual**, Senior Vice President at IHS Markit, Former US Ambassador to Mexico and Ukraine, and Special Envoy and Coordinator for International Energy Affairs at the State Department's Bureau of Energy and Natural Resources

Michael Ginsberg's book is designed for professionals looking for a concise guide to hydro, wind and PV practical applications. It is authoritative, yet easy to read and should be an essential primer for entrants to the renewable energy industry. I highly recommend it.

> —**Vasilis M. Fthenakis**, PhD, Senior Scientist Emeritus at the U.S. Department of Energy's Brookhaven National Laboratory, Founder and Director of the Center for Life Cycle Analysis at Columbia University, and a recipient of the 2018 William R. Cherry Award from the Institute of Electrical & Electronics Engineers

All renewable energy and business-focused professionals will benefit from this new book that is inclusive of a number of current and future energy options from solar and wind to fuel cells. It contains excellent case studies that will advance your knowledge of this critical subject.

> —**Robert J. Farrauto**, PhD, Professor of Professional Practice in the Earth and Environmental Engineering Department at Columbia University, and Former VP of R&D at BASF

Ginsberg's combination of an academic and practitioner makes this book an excellent resource for understanding the history and origin of renewable energy, including its current status and future trends.

> —**Ibrahim Odeh**, PhD, MBA, Director and Founder of the Global Leaders in Construction Management Research Initiative at Columbia University, and Advisory Committee Member of the World Economic Forum

I read Ginsberg's book and was impressed by how he incorporates all sides of the global renewable energy spectrum. I learned a lot!
>—**Sean White**, Solar Energy Professor, Consultant, Author, and 2014 Interstate Renewable Energy Council Trainer of the Year

Forewords

At a time when energy systems must shift rapidly from fossil fuels to renewable energy, Michael Ginsberg has produced an enormously valuable guide to renewable energy for practitioners, students, and the broad public. Ginsberg explains the concepts of renewable energy and project development with great clarity and insight, and offers illuminating case studies to enable readers to get to the nitty-gritty regarding the design and economics of renewable energy projects. This book will be widely adopted as renewable energy investments are rapidly scaled up around the world.

The book arrives at a moment of decision for the world. Human-induced climate change is proceeding rapidly and dangerously. Around the world, climate-related disasters—heatwaves, floods, droughts, extreme storms, rising sea levels—are causing vast damages and loss of lives and livelihoods. In the 2015 Paris Climate Agreement, the world's government determined to limit global warming to 1.5-degrees C relative to the pre-industrial average, yet average warming is already 1.1-degree C above the pre-industrial level and is rising by around 0.2-degree C per decade.

The most important step to achieving the 1.5-degree limit will be to decarbonize the world's energy system by mid-century. This will entail a worldwide shift in primary energy from fossil fuels to zero-carbon primary energy sources, the most important of which will be wind, solar, hydroelectric, geothermal, and nuclear power. In turn, downstream users of energy, such as transport and buildings, will shift from direct combustion of fossil fuels to electrification, such as with battery electric vehicles. Yet the transition to variable renewable energy sources, mainly wind and solar power, presents novel challenges in planning, design, grid management, technology selection, project development, and financing. It is on these crucial and practical issues that Ginsberg focuses, and on which he delivers with clarity and insight.

As Ginsberg vividly describes, variable renewable energy raises countless challenges of energy intermittency, choices of integrating with the grid or opting for stand-alone power generation, and various methods of financing. By working through specific case studies, with straightforward and illuminating numerical examples, Ginsberg offers the readers the tools for project analysis that will be vital for the widespread uptake of renewable energy. He also underscores many of the challenges ahead. Integrating variable renewable energy into the world's energy system will pose rising costs and challenges as the penetration of variable renewable energy rises. Yet the world will soon have to reach very high levels of renewable energy penetration in the near future in order to achieve the urgent climate goals set in Paris.

The transformation from fossil fuels to renewable energy will be the largest globally agreed technological overhaul ever undertaken. In view of the rapid advances in renewable energy technologies and systems design, the shift is feasible yet highly challenging. Michael Ginsberg's insightful book will provide important guidance along the way.

Jeffrey D. Sachs, a world-renowned professor of economics, leader in
sustainable development, and senior UN advisor

At long last, over the past decade renewable energy is finally receiving major global attention, action, and deployment in many countries, both developed and developing. This is happening at a critical time in human history, because the crisis in global climate change, driven primarily by anthropogenic CO_2 emissions produced by the relentless acceleration of human mining and utilization of fossil fuels over the past 100 years, is rapidly reaching a point of no return; that is, when the worst consequences of climate change cannot be avoided if a "business as usual" scenario continues.

This book by Michael Ginsberg, carefully and understandably presents the history, basic science and technology of renewable energy, along with the associated economic realities of commercialization, energy policy issues, and large-scale global implementation of the present most developed and impactful renewable energy technologies (wind, photovoltaics, hydropower, fuel cells, and advanced batteries).

Of particular interest is the discussion of modernization of the electrical power grid to accommodate the future large-scale input, storage, and distribution of renewable sources of electricity.

This book will be a valuable resource for those who are interested in the present and future role of renewable energy in society.

Arthur J. Nozik,
Professor of Chemistry, University of Colorado, Boulder and
Senior Research Fellow, Emeritus, National Renewable
Energy Laboratory, Golden, CO

Electricity from sunlight, hydropower and wind is on the rise. Cost reductions enabled by technological improvements and economies of scale have made renewable energy affordable and, in many cases, less expensive than conventional generation. Wind, and especially solar energy, are poised to become major contributors of our electricity mix by the mid-2050s or earlier.

Achieving this shift, however, requires careful planning, intelligent foresight, and an educated society. In this book, Michael Ginsberg, a member of my team at Columbia University researching grid integration, and an experienced renewable energy professional, synthesizes the key technical and management knowledge enabling the transformation of the electric grid.

Clear and concise, this book will advance public knowledge of renewable energy. It skillfully threads the most important engineering concepts with business and financial strategies, all of which are illustrated through practical case studies.

Renewable energy is freely distributed across our planet. The combination of technological advances in harnessing it, and political foresight in using it, open a clear path to a solution for our climate change and energy security challenges.

Vasilis M. Fthenakis, Senior Scientist Emeritus at the U.S.
Department of Energy's Brookhaven National Laboratory,
Founder and Director of the Center for Life Cycle Analysis
at Columbia University, and a recipient of the 2018
William R. Cherry Award from the Institute of
Electrical & Electronics Engineers

Acknowledgments

There are many individuals whom have supported this book. I am indebted to Krystyna Larkham, a talented communications specialist and scientist. She provided superb research and editorial assistance, and created many of the illustrations. In addition, I am grateful to Richard Driscoll, former branch chief of the Office of Global Change at the U.S. Department of State, and to Elie Kallab, fellow at the UN Sustainable Solutions Development Network, for their input and editorial support.

I am thankful to my advisor Dr. Vasilis Fthenakis, for guiding my research and providing the conceptual direction for this book. I am thankful to Dr. Jeffrey Sachs for his encouragement and for seeing this book's potential toward achieving deep decarbonization of global energy systems. I am thankful to Drs. Robert Farrauto and Daniel Esposito, for their mentorship and inspiring in me an appreciation of R&D and the hydrogen economy.

Thank you to Tim Stufft and Jose Aponte Aquino, my longtime friends and colleagues, and to Susan Gillum Smith, training specialist in the Department of State Bureau of Overseas Building Operations, who guided me as a trainer and communicator. I am grateful for Chris Izydore and Dr. Ibrahim Odeh, who imparted their insights into the construction industry. Thank you to Dr. Kenneth Walz, Principal Investigator of the Center for Renewable Energy Advanced Technological Education and Director of the Renewable Energy Program at Madison Area Technical College, Cris Folk, wind energy guru, and Dr. Sean White, solar master trainer and author of numerous books, for supporting my education in renewable energy technologies. I appreciate Urban Green Energy and Mateo Chaskel for the introduction to wind energy. Thank you to Dr. Damian Sciano, Director of Distributed Resource Integration at Con Edison, for his insights into utility operations and transmission and distribution systems. Thanks to my colleague Shahar Goeta, for his keen analytical review of the computations and scientific notation in this book.

I am fortunate to have had the incredible support of my family. In particular, I would like to thank Michael Roach, my grandfather and long-time mentor, who always encouraged me to pursue a sustainable future. His expertise in microgrids was invaluable. Finally, I would like to thank my husband Jeffrey Hanley, for his unending patience and support of this book and my other academic endeavors, and for expanding the horizons of my personal and professional aspirations.

Preface

Learning should be enjoyable, not laborious. It is an investment in oneself. Taking the time to learn is like putting money in the bank, while rewards may not be immediately realized, new knowledge lays the foundation for a better future for oneself, one's family, and the world.

It is in this spirit that I write this book. Reading a book or taking a class is like downloading someone's brain. A well-explained concept saves you copious time to reach that "aha" moment of understanding.

This book can be used in two ways, for self-learners and as a classroom textbook. Chapters are self-contained yet complementary. The most important concepts are italicized and each chapter contains a glossary with key terms. Questions at the end of each chapter are designed for the classroom and an Answers Manual complements this book for instructors. Online resources mentioned for this book are available on BEP's website at www.businessexpertpress.com. The book assumes no prior knowledge, but every reader should learn something new.

As someone who stumbled into engineering and science later in life, after intending a career in policy, I have distilled the most important concepts for policymakers and business professionals. I strongly believe that in today's complicated and complex world, where specialization prevents us from knowing everything and the stakes of ignorance have never been greater, the public needs to understand the science and technology that moves our world.

Plainly, engineers, scientists, policymakers, and businesspeople need to understand each other. This book seeks to break people out of their silos. Engineering without context is like a brain without a heart, and policy without engineering is like a heart without a brain. Neither function well individually. Understanding formulas without intent is just as ineffective as philosophers without practical skills.

A final note for the math-phobic: It is a shame that math steers so many away from STEM. Just like writing, math is a skill that can be improved and polished, at any age. A good friend and trainer once told me to be patient with yourself. It is a good mantra to keep in mind. Be kind to yourself, if it doesn't click right away it will in time. Now let's dive in.

Introduction

Why Renewable Energy?

We live at a critical time. Historians will look back at the 21st century as one in which decisions were made to either protect the planet and our quality of life, or set us on an irreversible downward spiral.

The 20th century was a time of remarkable advancement. In the span of 100 years we learned how to acclimatize our homes, power vehicles and planes, extend our lives, and communicate across the world instantaneously. This century is about advancing those movements sustainably, "meet(ing) the needs of the present without compromising the ability of future generations to meet their own needs."[1]

Electricity, despite its ubiquity, is an astoundingly new technology, and to make sustainable advancements we all need to understand how it works. Just because something is the way it is does not mean it must continue to be so in the future. Our electrical system is miraculous, but it is broken. It relies on burning old fossils that take millions of years to decompose. Why not use the sun and other abundant, practically endless resources? We can. Despite the myriad challenges and 'institutional inertia, the feeling of let's keep doing it this way because we always have,' we are in the midst of the greatest transformation our electrical system has ever seen. We are all part of the evolution of the electrical grid.

Beyond the grid, the transportation sector will require a major shift. The exploration of hydrogen fuel cells and batteries in this book lays the foundation for the deep decarbonization of our society in every sector toward a truly emissions-free society.

Reference

1. World Commission on Environment and Development. 1987. *Our Common Future*. Oxford: Oxford University Press.

Outline

Chapter 1: Historical and Conventional Power Production ("The Context")

To understand where we are going, we begin with where we came from by reviewing electrical theory and history.

Chapter 2: Renewable Energy Technologies ("The What")

We examine the operation of the primary renewable energy technologies, hydropower, wind energy, and solar energy. Also, we examine hydrogen fuel cells and batteries.

Chapters 3 to 5: Project Development Models ("The How")

We discuss models for the integration of renewable energy.

Chapter 6: The Emerging Renewable Energy Future ("The Transformation")

We look to the future, both the obstacles and opportunities.

CHAPTER 1

Historical and Conventional Power Production

I couldn't have electricity in the house, I wouldn't sleep a wink. All those vapors floating about.

—Dowager Countess Violet Grantham, Downton Abbey

It may seem hard to believe, but electricity is a new development. Only 100 years ago it was a terrifying idea to have the "power of lightning" in your home. We could compare this to the early 2000s when sharing personal information online became commonplace through platforms like Facebook, or today how it has become acceptable to get into a stranger's car for a ride. Only 20 years ago both of these concepts would have been frightening propositions. Yet today, information and car sharing, like electricity, are accepted as normal parts of life. We notice when electricity is not working, but do we even know how this "magical" force works?

How Do We Get Electricity?

For a long time, people knew there were invisible forces about. We could observe lightning and that somehow certain metals attracted or reflected one another. The combination of these two forces, electricity and magnetism, is called electromagnetism. Together, they give rise to the movement of electrons through a wire.

All elements are made up of atoms with protons and neutrons at their nucleus, and electrons in "orbits," swirling about their nucleus like planets around the sun, as show in Figure 1.1. These sub-atomic particles have charges. Protons are positive, electrons negative, and neutrons have no charge, so are neutral (although they do contribute to the atom's weight, as shown in Table 1.1).

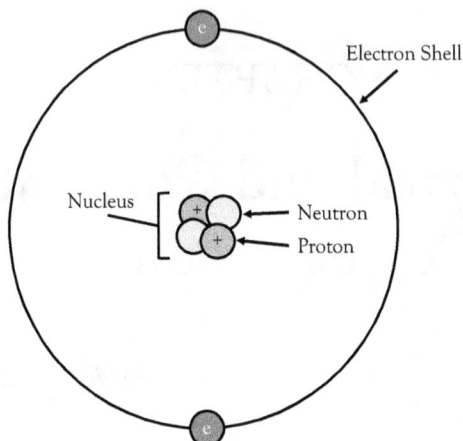

Figure 1.1 Atomic model of a helium atom, showing positions and charges of neutrons, protons and electrons.

Table 1.1 Charges and masses of subatomic particles

Subatomic particle	Charge	Relative mass
Proton	+	1
Neutron	0	1
Electron	−	0

Since opposites attract, negatively-charged electrons are held close to the nucleus by the force of their attraction to the positively-charged protons found there.

Electricity is the free flow of electrons through a conductor, or wire. We put those electrons to work when they power our *loads,* such as lights and motors. But if electrons are held in orbits by the force of attraction, how can we get them to flow freely to create electricity? That scientific breakthrough was made in 1800 by Italian Physicist Alessandro Volta, who discovered that if you introduce an external charge to an atom you can "eject" stable electrons out of their orbits and use them in a circuit.

His battery, known as a "Voltaic Pile," stacked together discs of zinc and copper, separated by blotting paper soaked in brine. The zinc had a chemical reaction with the water in the blotting paper, known as *reduction-oxidation (redox).* The zinc oxidized, each atom of zinc lost two electrons that were then free to move as current through a circuit. This was a huge breakthrough in the history of electricity. Previous experiments had used friction to generate current, but the Voltaic Pile was the first battery that could supply free electrons for a circuit.[1]

Similar to water flow, electrons flow by "pump pressure," or a _voltage source_, through a "pipe," or _conductor_. Along the way those electrons encounter _resistance_, like obstructions on a path, and serve our _loads_. The electrons give up some of their energy by powering our loads and return to the voltage source. In Figure 1.2, when the switch is closed, wires conduct, moving electrons (electricity) from the voltage source (battery) to the _electrical load_ (light bulb) and then back to the voltage source, encountering resistance along the way.

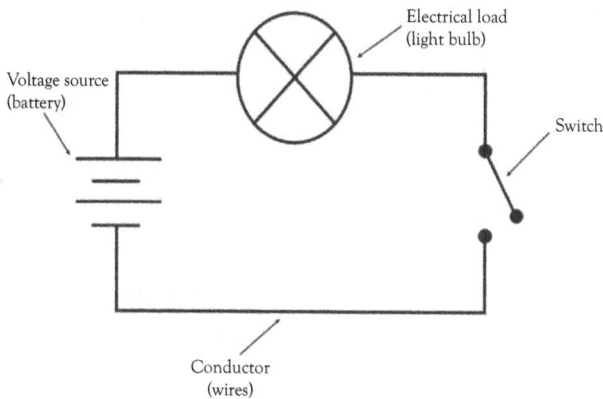

Figure 1.2 Simple electrical circuit showing a voltage source (battery), conductor (wires) and an electrical load (light).

These components of electricity, Voltage (V), Current (I) and Resistance (R), interact with each other in a relationship discovered by the 18th century German Physicist, George Ohm.

$$V = IR$$

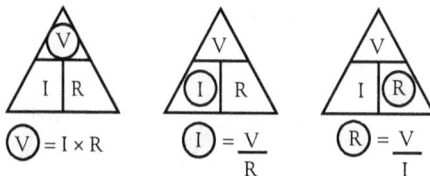

Figure 1.3 Ohm's Law triangle. To solve for the missing variable cover it up with your finger.

Voltage, the electrical potential, is the product of *current* and *resistance*. The electrical potential of a circuit is based on its current (the flow of electrons), and its resistance (how hard it is for the electrons to flow). *Resistance* represents electrical potential "lost" in the form of heat.

Basic Circuit Types

Series—in a series circuit, the current flows along one path. In Figure 1.4, the resistors, which may be lamps, are placed *in series*. In a series circuit, the total resistance is the sum of the individual resistances.

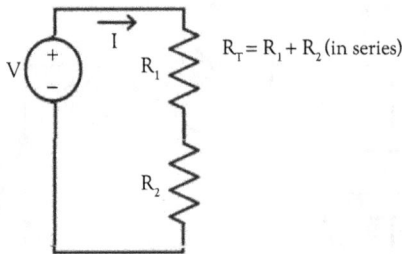

$$R_T = R_1 + R_2 \text{ (in series)}$$

Figure 1.4 **A series circuit showing two resistors connected to a voltage source.**

For instance, let's say you have a series circuit where the voltage is 12 volts, resistor 1 (R_1) is 50 ohms and resistor 2 (R_2) is 150 ohms. To find the total resistance (R_T) you add the two resistors:

$$R_1 + R_2 = 200 \text{ ohms}$$

To find the current, using Ohm's Law, I = V/R, thus:

$$I = 12 \text{ volts}/200 \text{ ohms}$$
$$= .06 \text{ amps} * 1000 \text{ milli-amps}/\text{amp}$$
$$= 60 \text{ milli-amps (mA)}$$

In a series circuit, the total voltage is the sum of the individual voltages. An important concept in a series circuit is that if there is a fault with one load the entire circuit is open and all subsequent loads will not be powered (think of Christmas lights).

Parallel—on the other hand, a circuit that has multiple branches allows current to flow in branches parallel to those with faults. In a parallel circuit, like the one shown in Figure 1.5, the total resistance is the sum of the reciprocal of each resistance. This means that the total resistance is always less than the smallest individual resistance. This makes sense because more paths for electrons to flow means greater current. Greater current means less resistance, and indeed total current in a parallel circuit is the sum of the individual branch currents.

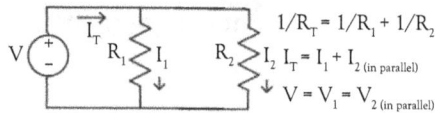

$$1/R_T = 1/R_1 + 1/R_2$$
$$I_T = I_1 + I_2 \text{ (in parallel)}$$
$$V = V_1 = V_2 \text{ (in parallel)}$$

Figure 1.5 A parallel circuit showing two resistors in parallel branches connected to a voltage source.

Let's take an example. If R_1 is 2 ohms and R_2 is 3 ohms, then the R_T is 1/2 ohms + 1/3 ohms:

$$1/R_T = 3/6 \text{ ohms} + 2/6 \text{ ohms}$$
$$= 5/6 \text{ ohms}$$

Taking the reciprocal of $1/R_T$, the total resistance is thus:

$$6/5 \text{ ohms}$$
$$= 1.2 \text{ ohms}$$

Finding the total current, we would use Ohm's Law, I = V/R. If the voltage is 6 volts, then:

$$I = 6 \text{ volts}/1.2 \text{ ohms}$$
$$= 5 \text{ amps}$$

Given the branch currents, and that the voltage is the same across branches, an easier way to determine total resistance is to find the individual branch currents, sum them, and then find the total resistance, as shown below.

$$V = IR \rightarrow I_T = V/R_T \rightarrow I_T = V/R_1 + V/R_2$$

$$I_1 = V/R_1 = 6 \text{ volts}/2 \text{ ohms} = 3 \text{ amps}$$

$$I_2 = V/R_2 = 6 \text{ volts}/2 \text{ ohms} = 2 \text{ amps}$$

$$I_T = I_1 + I_2 = 3 \text{ amps} + 2 \text{ amps} = 5 \text{ amps}$$

$$R_T = 6 \text{ volts}/5 \text{ amps} = 1.2 \text{ ohms}$$

What About Magnetism?

On closer examination, the flow of electrons within a conductor is based not just on the repulsion and attraction of electrons, but on their interaction with *magnetic fields*. Magnets are elements with intrinsic properties that give them a *magnetomotive force (mmf)* similar to the voltage pressure in an electrical circuit. There are several conditions that must be met for a material to be magnetic, but they all result in the same thing: the material must be capable of aligning all its magnetic *domains* in the same direction, as shown in Figure 1.6.

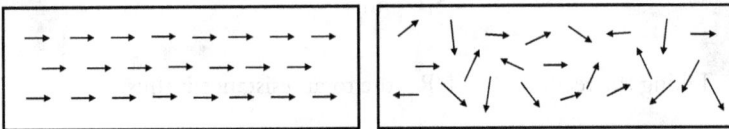

Magnetic substance with all domains in alignment   Non-magnetic substance with domains out of alignment

Figure 1.6 The alignment of domains in a magnetic substance and misalignment of domains in a non-magnetic substance.

Electricity and magnetism can be transformed into one another. Electricity and magnetism are linked, resulting in the term *electromagnetism*. In Figure 1.7, you can see that if you run current through a wire, it generates an electromagnetic field. But it also works the other way: if you move a wire through an electromagnetic field, the field causes the electrons to move, generating current.

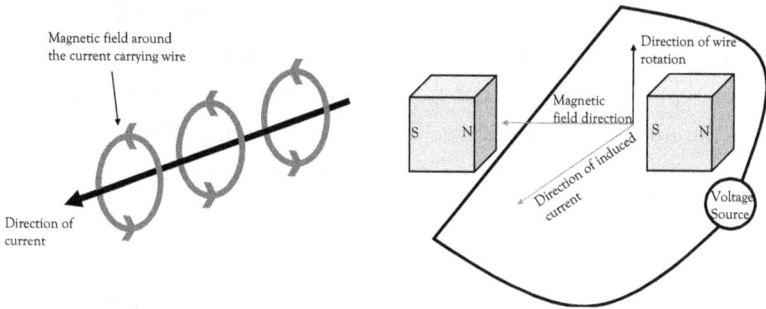

Figure 1.7 *Generation of a magnetic field around a current-carrying wire, and the electromagnetic induction of current when a wire moves through a magnetic field.*

How Is Voltage Generated?

Voltage is simply the amount of *flux*, "magnetic stuff," a conductor can capture over time. *Flux* is the magnetic field, the strength of which is determined by the magnetic material, over a certain area. To get more voltage, add more field, area, or windings (turns of the conductor coil). The degree to which a conductor interacts with the <u>magnetic flux</u> in its vicinity is called the <u>flux linkage</u>. If you are a science fiction geek like me, upon hearing the term flux you may have thought of the flux capacitor from Back to the Future—who knows, perhaps someday we will discover flux can warp the space-time continuum!

Voltage is Generated from Field

- **Voltage** = Energy/unit charge (Joules/coulomb)
  = **Electromotive force (EMF, or E)**

  - How much **electromagnetic potential** *"stuff"* captured by coils

$$\varepsilon = -N\,\frac{\Delta\Phi}{\Delta t}$$

Rate of change in magnetic flux

A coil captures field lines passing through an area.

N = Number of coil turns
Δ = **Change (delta)**
Φ = Flux ("magnetic stuff") (weber)
T = Time (seconds)

Φ = B*A
B = Magnetic field (tesla)
A = Area (meters squared)

Voltage induced determined by:
- Amount of field
- Area/orientation
- **Number of coils–how transformers work**

Figure 1.8 *Generation of voltage from a magnetic field.*

Michael Faraday's Law of induction, demonstrated in Figure 1.8, shows us that the amount of voltage generated on a coil is based on the amount of magnetic flux a current-carrying conductor captures over time, and the number of conductors. The more flux, the greater the induced voltage. The more coils, the greater the induced voltage.

Rules of Thumb

Power Rule: Similar to the Ohm's Law triangle. As shown in Figure 1.9, just cover up the missing variable to solve.

$$Power = Voltage * Current$$

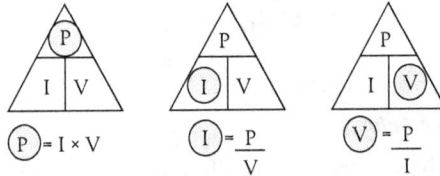

Figure 1.9 The power law triangle.

Ohm's Law Wheel: Combining Ohm's Law and the Power Law. Cover up the variable you seek in the inner circle (P, V, I or R), and solve using one of the three equations in the respective quarter circle.

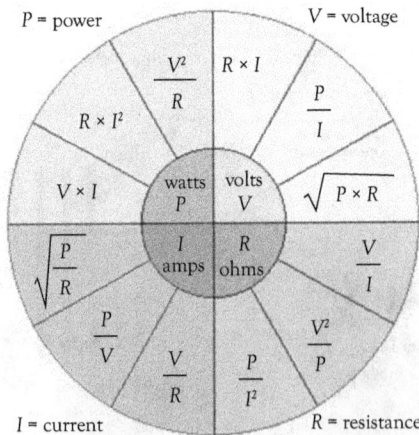

Figure 1.10 Ohm's law wheel.

Source: Wikimedia Commons[2]

A Note on Calculations: Railway Method (Dimensional Analysis) for Units Conversion

Always remember the units! Engineers must convert units all the time, and most errors are made from unit conversions gone wrong. In order to ensure we are clear on units, the *railway method*, so-called because the multiplication and division symbols come together to look like train tracks, is a simple way of converting. Note we always write out the units and treat them as factors that can be cancelled.

For instance, if we want to convert 10 feet into inches:

Conversion Factor: 1 foot = 12 inches

$$\frac{10 \ \text{feet}}{} \ \Bigg| \ \frac{12 \ \text{inches}}{1 \ \text{foot}}$$

*The feet cancel and we are left multiplying 10 * 12 = 120 inches.*

Should there be more or less inches than the equivalent in feet? More! Because there are 12 inches in 1 foot. Also, we should be left with the unit inches.

When dealing with multiple unit conversions this method is very useful. For instance, if we want to convert 3.5 yards to millimeters (mm):

Conversion Factors:
1 yard = 3 feet
1 foot = 12 inches
1 inch = 25.4 mm

$$\frac{3.5 \ \text{yards}}{} \ \Bigg| \ \frac{3 \ \text{feet}}{1 \ \text{yard}} \ \Bigg| \ \frac{12 \ \text{inches}}{1 \ \text{foot}} \ \Bigg| \ \frac{25.44 \ \text{mm}}{1 \ \text{inch}}$$

Therefore, we have 3.5 * 3 * 12 * 25.44 = 3200.4 mm.

Common sense check: There are 3 feet in a yard, 12 inches in a foot, and many mm in an inch, so we should end up with a much larger number. Check! The yards, feet, and inches should cancel out, and we should be left with mm. Check!

The Commercialization of Direct Current Electricity

In the span of human history, electricity has only been around for the blink of an eye, and its tale is storied. Consider the "War of Currents" between Thomas Edison and Nicola Tesla. The story begins with a young Tesla working for Edison, and ends with Edison purportedly electrocuting animals to prove the dangers of high voltage *Alternating Current* (AC).

Figure 1.11 **Left: Thomas Edison, inventor of the indoor incandescent light bulb and defender of Direct Current, and right, Nikola Tesla, inventor of Alternating Current and the AC motor.**

Source: Library of Congress[3]

Industry was quick to realize the potential of "harnessed electricity." In 1878, Edison produced the indoor incandescent light. At the time, batteries and *Direct Current* (DC) generators were being used to power arc lighting systems, which is luminescent gas ignited by a pulse of voltage, and, believe it or not, battery-powered electric vehicles.

By 1882, Edison was providing electrical power to 59 customers in Manhattan, upending the incumbent gas light utilities. However, long-distance transmission of Edison's DC supply was proving impractical.

Edison asked a young Serbian employee, Nicola Tesla, to solve this problem. Unfortunately for Edison, Tesla's research led him to believe that DC would never work for mass electrification. In DC production, the electrons pushed out by a power station are the same ones that enter customers' lights and machines, requiring loads to be as close as possible to the voltage source to reduce power loss.

Tesla's solution was to make the electrons in conductors "jiggle" back and forth, delivering power without themselves traveling to each customer. With AC, Tesla figured that electricity could be generated away from population centers and sent over great distance.

Transforming AC Voltage

Twinkle Twinkle Little Star, Power Equals I Squared R: Recall Ohm's Law Wheel. We use AC power to transmit electricity over great distances since it can be easily transformed to have high voltage and low current. Greater current means more power loss due to friction requiring larger wires, so we use AC power to reduce the current and reduce power loss and costs.

- AC voltage is easily transformed, making it convenient to send over large distances.
- AC power can be sent in 3 phases, maximizing the amount of power delivered to the load.
- The size of a wire is related to its ability to conduct current.
- Like water in a pipe, a smaller wire can carry less current than a larger wire. Larger wires mean more material and cost.

By generating electricity at a low voltage, and then using a step-up transformer to increase the voltage and decrease the current, we can use smaller wires to transmit power over great distances, and reduce heat loss.

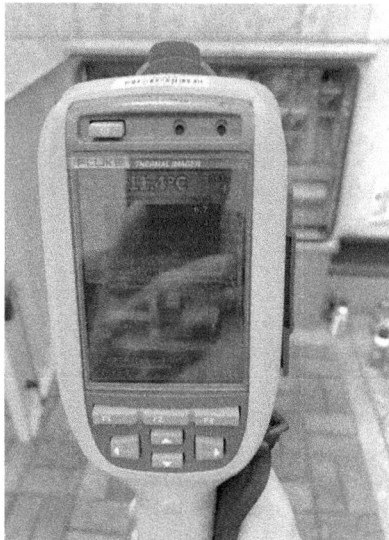

Figure 1.12 Thermal imaging of an electrical panel, demonstrating a wire's ability to conduct current and the resulting heat loss. Photo by author.

Tesla, who today is known as the inventor of the AC motor and the modern system of electrical power generation and transmission, had a vision of electricity in every home and he understood that to make this happen, great amounts of power would be needed.[4] At the time, batteries were limited and expensive, but a new technology, the engine in motors and generators, was being rolled out on a large scale.

The Operation of Motors and Generators

Driven by fuel combustion as its *prime mover*, the engine in a car combusts fuel to turn a rotor that propels the vehicle. This engine could also be used to generate AC electric power as part of a generator. A generator is comprised of a rotor (rotating part) and a stator (stationary part). Mechanical power is transferred to electrical power by an engine turning the moving rotor and using *induction* to pass off the _electromotive force_ in the rotor to wires in the stator to produce electricity.

Recall from Faraday's Law of induction—an electromagnet produces a magnetic field. When a coil passes through that field it generates current on the wire. When current passes through a coil it generates a field. The field induces a voltage on other coils. In a generator like the one shown in Figure 1.13, a field on the rotor windings induces a voltage and current in the stator windings. In a transformer, primary coils produce a field that induces a voltage in secondary coils.

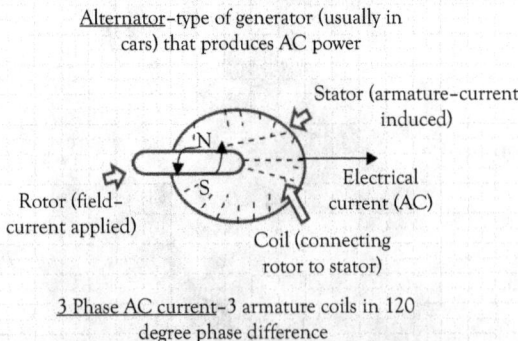

Alternator-type of generator (usually in cars) that produces AC power

Stator (armature–current induced)

N

S

Electrical current (AC)

Rotor (field– current applied)

Coil (connecting rotor to stator)

3 Phase AC current-3 armature coils in 120 degree phase difference

Figure 1.13 Diagram of an Alternator producing AC electrical power.

This moving rotor creates a sine wave that produces the "jiggling" motion of the AC electrons, constantly moving back and forth between positive and negative voltage and current.

The windings that initiate energy transfer are known as *field windings*. The windings that receive energy are known as *armature windings*. In a generator, electrical feeders run from the stator to the switchboard where the electricity is directed to loads.

The First Law of Thermodynamics states that energy cannot be created nor destroyed, only transformed. Generators convert mechanical energy to electrical energy, passing the energy of the moving rotor to the stator. Motors work by the same principle, just in reverse—electrical energy is transformed into mechanical energy. In a motor, electricity in the stator generates a field that moves a rotor.

Power always flows from field windings to armature windings. In a motor, the field windings are located in the stator and the armature windings are in the rotor. In a generator, the field windings are in the rotor and the armature windings are in the stator. In the following diagram, "mechanical parts" are the rotor and stator, think of them as the physical equipment, and "electrical parts" are the field and armature windings. The parts are the same in both a motor and generator, the only difference is the flow of energy.

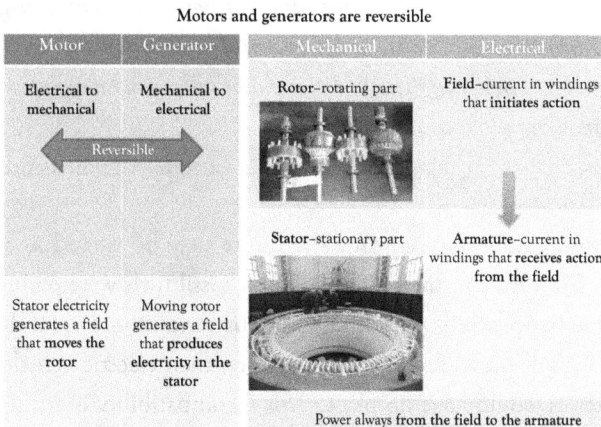

Motors and generators are reversible

Motor	Generator	Mechanical	Electrical
Electrical to mechanical	Mechanical to electrical	Rotor–rotating part	Field–current in windings that initiates action
	Reversible		
		Stator–stationary part	Armature–current in windings that receives action from the field
Stator electricity generates a field that moves the rotor	Moving rotor generates a field that produces electricity in the stator		

Power always from the field to the armature

Figure 1.14 Reversibility of motors and generators. The windings are copper or aluminum. The electromagnetic core is iron. Image sources: Various types of rotors (Wikimedia Commons) and Stator for hydroelectric power plant (Wikimedia Commons).

The Commercialization of AC Electricity

Around the same time as Edison was pushing DC lighting, the industrialist George Westinghouse was researching AC and transformers. By the mid-1880s, Westinghouse had developed the induction coil for AC power transformation, and the fight between AC and DC, or the "War of Currents" was in full swing.

Westinghouse bought some of Tesla's patents, and began installing AC generators around the U.S., expanding AC electricity to remote areas Edison could not reach, and undercutting Edison in areas where he was already established. With his business under threat, Edison turned his efforts to depicting AC as a technology with dangerously high voltages. He secretly funded an inventor to use AC in his design for an electric chair, and used high voltage AC electricity to execute dogs, calves and horses. It was still Westinghouse, however, who won the coveted contract to power the 1893 Chicago World Fair, using Tesla's AC electricity.[5]

Another Perspective on Why Edison Was Against Alternating Current

Electricity is the thing. There are no whirring and grinding gears with their numerous levers to confuse. There is not that almost terrifying uncertain throb and whirr of the powerful combustion engine. There is no water circulating system to get out of order—no dangerous and evil-smelling gasoline and no noise.

—Thomas Edison

In retrospect, Edison's vision for the future may be viewed as ahead of his time. Even back in the 1900s, he knew fossil fuels were polluting our environment. Solar cells produce DC and batteries store DC. If the future was to be built on AC and fuel generators, then electric vehicles, solar, and batteries would have no place. This incompatibility is at the crux of the current obstacles for many renewable energy sources. Clearly AC won the "War of Currents." Today, developed countries have AC infrastructure and fossil fuels are the predominant source.

The Development of Electric Grids

Edison and Westinghouse ran early examples of private or _Investor-owned Utilities (IOUs)_. During the early 20th century, IOUs emerged throughout the country. At the same time in Europe, scientists and business owners were developing their own power stations and energy supply systems. Over time, companies cooperated with each other to balance the load on power stations and ensure full supply at peak times. Eventually, these systems merged into what we now call the "grid"– the integrated network of power stations and transmission infrastructure that provides consumers with electricity on demand.

USA

By the beginning of the 20th century, America had more than 4,000 individual private utility producers, greater in number and diversity than Europe. When these companies began to cooperate with each other in larger grid systems, the large size of the US and the diversity of geographies and providers led to the creation of three connected, yet distinct, electrical systems:

- The Eastern Interconnection (mostly east of the Colorado Rockies)
- The Western Interconnection (mostly west of the Colorado Rockies)
- The Electric Reliability Council of Texas

Within each system, smaller local grids were connected together and the flow of power managed by a _balancing authority_, an entity that coordinates electricity generation and transmission in a region.

The layout of the US electric grid was informed by a low population density, especially in rural areas, and high individual electrical loads. Energy from power stations is distributed throughout the U.S. via medium to high voltage _primary cables,_ or _transmission lines_. When these cables reach an area of population density/electrical load, a small distribution transformer is installed, often atop a pole above ground. _Secondary_ *cables,* or *distribution lines,* then conduct the stepped-down electricity to a few consumers over short distances. This grid pattern has a higher load capacity per mile of circuit compared to European grids, and is suited to America's large distances between energy consumers. There is a distribution transformer for every few houses and when new houses or other electrical loads are built, it is easy to add a new, small step-down transformer and secondary cables to the system.[6]

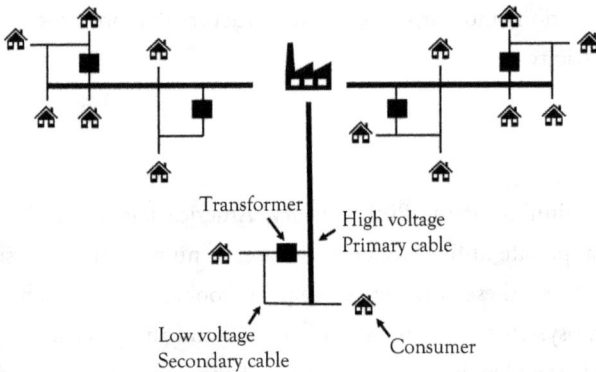

Figure 1.15 Schematic of the North American grid system.

Europe

Europe's small countries and political structures led to the rapid development of national energy boards, standardization of supply, and nationalization of each country's energy grid. In the UK, the first steps toward a standardized energy system were taken in 1919, and the national grid began operation in 1938. In France, the densely-connected national grid was nationalized in 1946.

Europe's dense population and lower load density than the U.S. meant that space was a commodity. Fewer step-down transformers were built and were usually placed underground or inside vaults. In Europe, electricity is carried to consumers via an extensive network of secondary, 220 volt underground cables. The use of 220 volts, as opposed to the 110 volts in the U.S., means the secondary lines can deliver power to customers farther from the step-down transformer. This means less transformers are needed. Also, higher voltage cables means less current and smaller (cheaper) wires can be used.

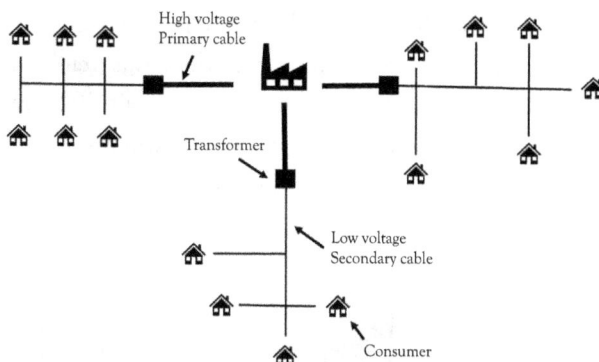

Figure 1.16 Schematic of the European grid system.

Both in the U.S. and Europe, a drive for greater profits through economies of scale pushed utilities to become *vertically-integrated* regional monopolies, owning all parts of the power supply chain—the generation, transmission, and distribution. Beginning in the late 1970s, however, regulators began to restructure utilities to lower the cost of electricity and encourage greater environmental protection from a diverse supply of generators. Today, many utilities no longer own the majority of their generation, and purchase their power through *power purchase agreements (PPAs)* with generators.

As part of this restructuring, the U.S. and Europe began to *deregulate* the electricity sector in the 1990s, allowing consumers to choose an electricity provider that generates or markets electricity other than their utility. In this case, the utility still owns and operates the transmission and distribution system. Deregulation was done, in part, to promote renewable energy adoption while reducing rates.

Renewable Energy on the Rise

There are three types of conventional generators. *Baseload* power is always on and forms the backbone of our energy supply. These sources are primarily nuclear power and combined cycle power plants. The next category is *cycling units*, mostly gas and oil steam plants. They alternate their output during the day and can ramp production up or down quickly over a range of 25 to 100 percent of their capacity. These cycling units provide the grid with flexibility and are particularly important for facilitating the integration of variable solar and wind resources. When demand spikes, a third category, *peaker* gas turbines are turned on and rapidly brought to full load.

Despite their variability, renewable energy is comprising an increasingly significant share of global energy production. This trend is intensifying. In 2017, 18 percent of all electricity in the U.S. came from renewable sources, up from 5 percent in 2015, and solar and wind projects made up 62 percent of new power generation investment.[8]

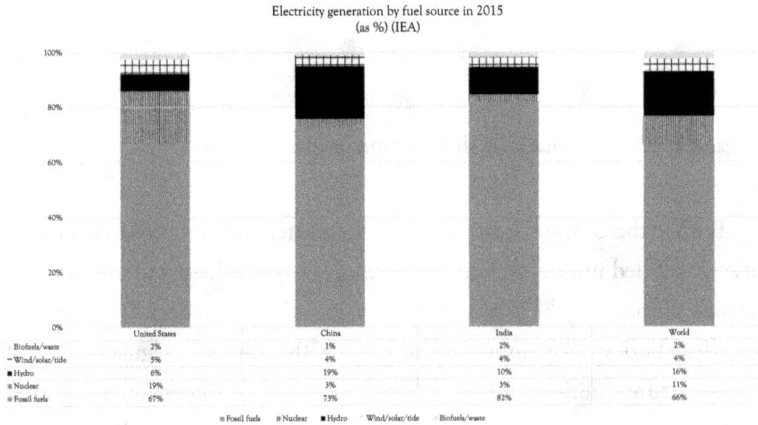

Electricity generation by fuel source in 2015
(as %) (IEA)

	United States	China	India	World
Biofuels/waste	2%	1%	2%	2%
Wind/solar/tide	5%	4%	4%	4%
Hydro	6%	19%	10%	16%
Nuclear	19%	3%	3%	11%
Fossil fuels	67%	73%	82%	66%

■ Fossil fuels   ■ Nuclear   ■ Hydro   Wind/solar/tide   Biofuels/waste

Figure 1.17 Electricity generation by fuel source in major countries and the world in 2015.

Source: IEA 2015. All Rights Reserved.[7]

Chapter 1 Questions

1. If the voltage in a series circuit is 12 with resistance 1 of 40 ohms and resistance 2 of 20 ohms, what is the current in milliamps (mA)?
2. In a parallel circuit, if the resistance of branch 1 is 4 ohms and the resistance of branch 2 is 2 ohms, and the voltage is 8, what is the current?
3. Using the railway method, convert 10 amps to milliamps (mA).
4. Using the Ohm's Law Wheel, how much power in watts is in a circuit with 10 amps of current and 12 ohms of resistance?
5. What is the voltage of a circuit with a 2.2 kilowatt power source and 20 ohms of resistance?
6. Explain how electricity is generated. What is meant by the reversibility of motors and generators?
7. Why do you think Edison ultimately lost the AC/DC power battle? Do you think there is any way that he could have succeeded?

Chapter 1 Glossary

Conductor: a material that electrons/current can flow through. Most conductors are metals.

Current: the free flow of electrons through a conductor or wire. Unit is amps.

Deregulation of Electricity: Consumers purchasing electricity from providers other than their utilities, although the utilities still own and operate the transmission and distribution system.

Electrical Load: the part of a circuit that draws or consumes electrical power.

Electromagnetism: the interaction between electric and magnetic fields.

Electromotive Force: the difference in electrical potential that results in an electric current.

Flux linkage: how much a conductor interacts with magnetic flux.

Magnetic Flux: The amount of magnetic field passing through a surface area.

Power: the amount of energy transferred (work) per unit of time. Unit is watts.

Power Purchase Agreement (PPA): A key element of project finance, the contract between an energy-generating party and an energy-buying party, setting out the cost of the power transferred.

Resistance: how difficult it is for electrons/current to flow through a conductor. Unit is ohms.

Voltage Source: analogous to a pump, the entity that creates the force to power electrons through a circuit.

Voltage: The size of the force powering electrons through a circuit. Also known as the difference in *electrical potential*. Unit is volts.

References

1. MIT Libraries logo MIT Libraries. n.d. https://libraries.mit.edu/collections/vail-collection/topics/electricity/the-voltaic-pile/
2. Wikimedia Commons. n.d. *Attribution: VampireBaru*, https://en.wikipedia.org/wiki/File:Ohm%27s_law_formula_wheel.JPG This file is licensed under the Creative Common Attribution-ShareAlike 3.0 Unported License.
3. Nicola, T. 1890. "Library of Congress." http://loc.gov/pictures/item/2014684845/

4. King, G. 2011. "Edison vs. Westinghouse: A Shocking Rivalry." *Smithsonian.com*, October 11, 2011. https://smithsonianmag.com/history/edison-vs-westinghouse-a-shocking-rivalry-102146036/ (accessed September 12, 2018).

5. "Tesla, Life and Legacy - War of the Currents." *PBS*, https://www.pbs.org/tesla/ll/ll_warcur.html

6. Von Meier, A. 2006. *Electric Power Systems a Conceptual Introduction*. Hoboken, NJ: Wiley-Interscience.

7. IEA Statistics. https://iea.org/statistics/?country=WORLD&year=2016&category=Energy%20supply&indicator=TPESbySource&mode=chart&dataTable=BALANCES

8. *2018 Sustainable Energy in America Factbook*. Report. Bloomberg New Energy Finance.

CHAPTER 2

Renewable Energy Technologies

I'd put my money on the sun and solar energy. What a source of power! I hope we don't have to wait till oil and coal run out before we tackle that.

—Thomas Edison

Now that we understand the historical development of electricity and dependence on fossil fuels, it is time to look to the role of renewable energy in reshaping the electric grid. In this chapter, we will review the science and applications of *hydropower, solar photovoltaics, wind turbines, hydrogen fuel cells,* and *batteries.*

Hydropower

It is fitting to begin with hydropower as it plays a pivotal role in the history of electrification. We have long dreamed of harnessing the power of rivers and waterfalls—and for centuries have successfully used water to power saw mills, flour mills and other mechanical machinery. But how do we turn this power into electricity?

In 1885, the Niagara Falls Commission was established to find a way to generate electricity from Niagara Falls, one of the world's most famous waterfalls. After the success of the 1893 World's Fair in Chicago, Westinghouse and Tesla were awarded a contract to develop an AC-generating hydropower plant at Niagara Falls. Despite the doubts of the private investors, Tesla's design was a success, and the first electricity generated by the Falls reached Buffalo, New York at midnight on November 16, 1896. In just a few years, AC electricity from Tesla's hydropower generator was powering New York City, and lighting up Broadway.[1]

How Hydropower Works

Figure 2.1 Smuggler-Union Hydroelectric Power Plant in Telluride, CO.
Source: Author

One of the earliest hydro plants in the U.S., the Bridalveil Falls Hydroelectric plant in Telluride, Colorado, shown in Figure 2.1, was built in 1907 to power nearby mining operations. It is still in use today, using its original 2,300 volt Westinghouse Electric AC generator, one of the oldest still in operation, to meet about 25 percent of the town of Telluride's electricity demand.

The waterfall cascades over 111 meters (365 ft). This height, also known as "hydraulic head," is a key determinant in the high power capacity of the plant (500 kW), generating approximately 1,700 MWh per year, according to the San Miguel Power Association.[2]

As demonstrated by the Bridalveil Falls plant, water at *height* contains a lot of energy. In fact, the *potential energy* (P.E.) of water depends on the mass of water, the acceleration of gravity, and the height, or head, of the water. To determine the P.E. of water, we must know two pieces of information—its *volume* in cubic meters (m³) and *height* in meters.

Potential Energy (P.E., joules) = m * g * h

m = mass of water (kilograms, kg)

g = acceleration of gravity, a constant of about 10 meters (m)/second²

h = height or head (meters). Distance from the water intake to the turbine.

$$Since\ density\ (d) = \frac{mass}{volume} \rightarrow mass = volume\ (V) * density$$

Substituting mass for V * d in the above formula, gives us:

P.E. = V * d * g * h

V = volume in m³
d = density of water, constant 1,000 kg/m³

Since the density of water is constant, we can simplify:

P.E. = 1,000 kg/m³ * 10 m/s² * V * h

P.E. = 10,000 Vh

The **power** from water is the rate that energy is used, which means that it is equal to the potential energy of the water over a unit of time.

Power (watts) = P.E./Time
(Also, from this we see Energy = Power * Time)

Using the formula in the box above, we can see that P.E./time = 10,000 Vh/Time. Volume/time is **flow** in m³/second.

Therefore, substituting flow for volume/time, we get:

Power = 10,000fh

f = flow (m³/second). How fast the water moves downstream.
h = height or head (meters). Distance from the water intake to the turbine.

Hydropower can be both large and small. Its size is classified by its power output, which is determined by the **flow** (m³/s) and the head, or **height**, of the source (m).

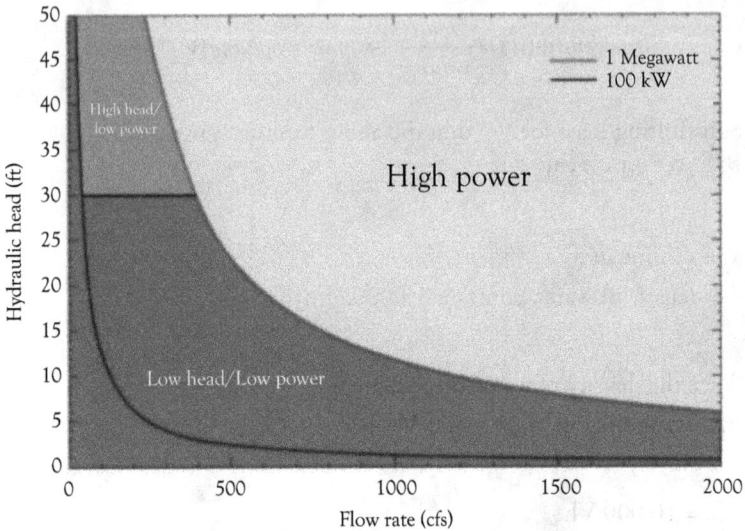

Figure 2.2 Hydroelectric power output as a function of hydraulic head and flow rate. The greater the hydraulic head and flow rate, the greater the power output.

Source: NREL

Determining the Power Output and Revenue of a Hydropower Plant

Let's take an example. You are a developer with a license to construct a large hydroelectric power plant capturing the energy of a local river, and you need to decide between two potential locations. The river has an average *flow* of 42 m³/s.

- At *Location 1,* a natural waterfall provides 20 meters of *head.*
- At *Location 2,* a proposed dam could provide 200 meters of *head.*

What is the **power**, in MW, produced at each location?

- 1 MW = 1,000,000 Watts
- 1 kW = 1,000 Watts
- Assume the efficiency is 90 percent (0.9)

Remember: **Power (Watts) = 10,000 * Flow (m³/s) * Height (m) * Efficiency Derating**

Location 1 Power Capacity = 10,000 * 42 m³/s * 20 m * 0.9
= 7,560,000 Watts/1,000,000 Watts/MW
= 7.56 MW

Location 2 Power Capacity = 10,000 * 42 m³/s * 200 m * 0.9
= 75,600,000 Watts/1,000,000 Watts/MW
= 75.6 MW

So, a hydroelectric plant at <u>Location 2</u> generates more power and, ignoring all other factors, is the better site.

Power v. Energy

Power output is referred to as *capacity*. As shown below, the *energy* produced from a system is different than its power capacity. Energy is power multiplied by time:

Energy (MWh) = Power (MW) * Time (hours)

Energy companies usually sell their energy to consumers in units of MWh, or kWH, so for a developer it is necessary to know the energy production of their plant to quantify revenue.

In quantifying revenue, we must also consider the *capacity factor*, or the percentage of time the system is running during the year, as there will always be downtime for maintenance.

Let's say your hydropower plant has a *power purchase agreement* (PPA) that a utility will buy the energy produced at $50/MWh. The five-year average *capacity factor* for U.S. conventional hydropower plants is 39 percent.[3] Assuming the *capacity factor* is 39 percent, what will be the plant's *revenue* at each potential location?

Revenue = Power Capacity * 24 hours/day * 365 days/year * capacity factor * MWh value

Location 1 Annual Revenue = 7.56 MW * 24 hours/day * 365 days/
year * 0.39 * $50/MWh = **$1,291,399.20**

Location 2 Annual Revenue = 75.6 MW * 24 hours/day * 365 days/year * 0.39 * $50/MWh = **$12,913,992.00**

Clearly, Location 2 has a much greater revenue potential!

Measuring Flow

It is clear that being able to measure the *flow* of water (volume/time) in a potential hydro resource is vital to calculating how much energy can be harnessed. But how do you do it? It all comes down to measuring the two key components of flow:

1. Volume of water (cubic meters, m^3/s)
2. Time (seconds, s)

Bucket Method

Find a bucket or another vessel with a known *volume*, place it in your flowing water source, and measure how much *time* it takes to fill. You can only do this with a small stream or other micro hydro system—imagine putting a bucket under Niagara Falls!

Float Method

For a larger body of flowing water like a stream or small river, measure the *width* and *depth* of the body of water, then toss a float in the water and measure the *time* it takes to travel a specific distance downstream. Then use the measurements to calculate flow.

$$\textbf{Flow} = m^3/time$$
$$= (width * depth * distance)/time$$

Salt Pump Method

Although the Salt Pump method works similarly to the Float method, it is more accurate as it measures flow at all depths of the hydro resource, not just on the surface. Measure the *width* and *depth* of the body of water, then release a specific amount of salt into it. Use special equipment to measure the concentration of salt at a specified *distance* downstream, and the *time* it took to get there.

Weir Method

This method is the most accurate way to measure flow as the *depth* and *width* of the flowing water are dictated by a human-made structure, not by nature. Measure the *width* of the weir, a low dam across a river, and then measure the *depth* of the water flowing over it. Use these two numbers in combination with a *weir table* to calculate the *flow.*[4, 5]

Inside a Hydropower Plant

Hydropower plants in the 21st century use exactly the same principles employed by Tesla at Niagara Falls to harness the power of water and turn it into electricity. Figure 2.3 outlines the key components of a modern hydropower plant.

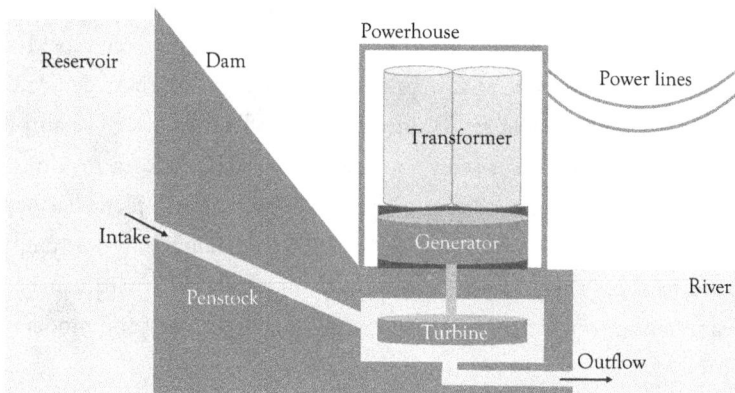

Figure 2.3 Cross section of a hydropower plant. Adapted from Tennessee Valley Authority under Wikimedia Commons.[6]

> *Dam*: How can you ensure a constant flow of water through your hydropower plant? By building a dam and creating a reservoir. This means that your power production will not be immediately affected by floods and droughts.
>
> *Intake, Control Gate, and Penstock*: Water flows out of the dam through the intake, and enters the Penstock, which transfers water to the Turbine. The hydropower plant can regulate the flow of water by lowering or raising the control gate.
>
> *Turbine*: The force of the water rotates the blades of the turbine. This rotation passes up the shaft to turn the large magnets in the generator.

Generator: Here is where the magic of electromagnetic induction happens. The rotating magnets (rotor) act on electrons in the coils of the stationary part of the generator (stator) and induce them to move, generating Alternating Current (AC).

Transformer: The transformer acts on the generated electricity, stepping up the voltage, and causing a proportional reduction in current. Now it is practical to send power across the country.

Power Lines: The current is conducted to consumers via power lines, either below ground or held aloft by pylons.[7]

Grounding: As with all power generators, a copper grounding wire must be used to direct short circuits or stray currents out of harm's way to the ground.

Hydropower plants can be installed almost anywhere there is running water. For instance, the author visited an 18 kW micro-hydro power plant in a remote area of the Colombian Sierra Nevadas. This plant was installed under a USAID Clean Energy Program dedicated to promoting the use of renewable energy in off-grid areas.[8] The author had the opportunity to survey the site[9] and learned the area previously relied on small diesel generators. The micro-hydropower plant has only been in operation for 8 years, but this off-grid camp now has ample power to meet the area's basic needs. When available, hydro can be a great renewable resource with an extremely high efficiency and moderate capacity factor.

It is important, however, to note there are issues with hydropower plants, specifically methane emissions and disruptions to aquatic ecosystems and human populations. Decisions to develop a hydropower plant should carefully consider these adverse consequences. Let's look at a case study.

Case Study: Three Gorges Dam

The Three Gorges Dam is the world's largest hydroelectric dam. It was built by China on the Yangtze River and went into operation in 2008. The Three Gorges Dam has a total installed generating capacity of 22,500 MW, surpassing the 14,000 MW of installed capacity at the Itaipú hydroelectric power plant on the Brazil and Paraguay border, which produced the most power from any hydro plant in the world in 2016. The largest hydroelectric power plant in the U.S. is the Grand Coulee Dam, which is located on the Columbia River, Washington, and has a generating capacity of about 6,800 MW (5th overall worldwide).[10]

The Three Gorges power units generated 93.53 TWh of electricity in 2016. This enormous dam is 181 meters (594 feet) in height and 2,335 meters (7,770 feet) in length; and behind it the Three Gorges Reservoir, has formed, with a surface area of about 1,045 square kilometers (400 square miles) and extends upstream from the dam about 600 kilometers (370 miles).[11]

In addition to generating electricity, the Three Gorges Dam provides flood control on the lower Yangtze River. The river has had catastrophic floods in 1931, 1935, 1954, and 1998, killing more than 300,000 people. The 1931 flood left an estimated 140,000 people dead and the 1954 flood around 30,000 people.[12] Further, the dam complex, with a series of locks and ship lifts, improve shipping and navigation on the Yangtze.[13]

The dam came at a substantial environmental and social price. Vast expanses of habitat were lost to the reservoir and more than 1.2 million residents along the Yangtze River were forced to relocate, most of whom are farmers lacking formal education. These displaced populations ended up in cities, many ill-equipped to support themselves.[14]

Lastly, dams are the leading source of methane due to human activities. Methane is a potent greenhouse gas that traps more heat than carbon dioxide. The methane emissions are due to the rotting of the trees, stumps, and vegetation flooded by reservoirs and the gas produced at the reservoir bottom is freed when it comes to the water surface or at the turbines and spillways. While it is uncertain how much methane is released at the Three Gorges reservoir, it is estimated to be substantial.[15]

Solar Photovoltaics

A ray of light…consists of a finite number of energy quanta local-
ized at points in space, moving without dividing and capable of
being absorbed or generated only as entities…the number of elec-
trons leaving the body will be proportional to the intensity of the
exciting light.

—1905, Heinrich Rudolf Hertz, Albert Einstein, *On*
a Heuristic Viewpoint Concerning the Production and
Transformation of Light

The Photoelectric Effect

The word photovoltaic (PV) is a combination of *photon*, particles of light
or electromagnetic radiation, and *voltaic*, production of electricity. Therefore, it describes the production of electricity from light.

Light is not a "beam" or a "ray." In fact it is a wave from a stream of
quantum particles or packets of energy called *photons*. When a photon
hits the surface of a material, the energy is absorbed and excites electrons
in the outer, or *valence*, shell of the atoms that make up the material.
In a *semiconductor*, these electrons may be dislodged as free photoelectrons,
as shown in Figure 2.4.

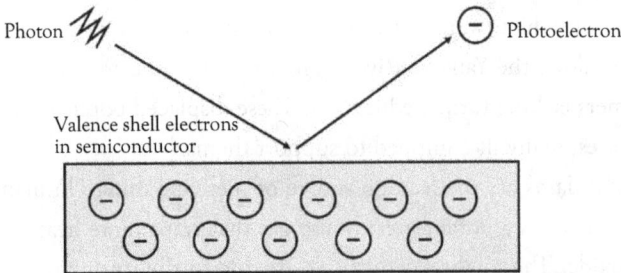

Figure 2.4 Diagram showing light waves hitting the surface of a
semiconductor and dislodging electrons to become free photoelectrons.

In a semiconductor, as shown in Figure 2.5, the energy of the photons
allows *valence shell* electrons to "jump" into the *conduction band*, which
are then free to work in an electric circuit.

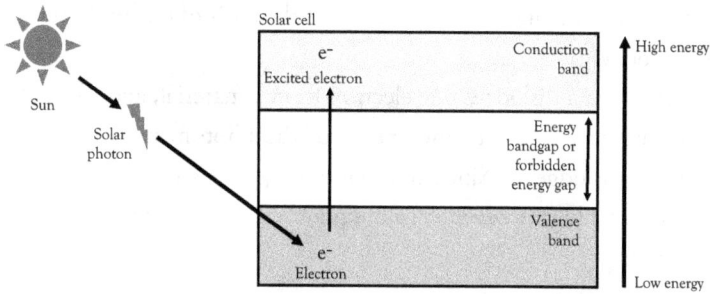

Figure 2.5 Light energy in the form of a solar photon hits the valence band within a semiconductor and excites an electron, which jumps across the "forbidden energy gap" to the conduction band to be used as current.

The Discovery of the Photoelectric Effect

In the late 1800s, a German physicist called Heinrich Hertz discovered that shining ultraviolet light on a metal surface resulted in a spark. English Physicist JJ Thompson identified that the spark was in fact electrons dislodged from valence shells inside the metal, and German physicist Philipp Lenard found that doubling the *intensity* of the light had no impact on the energy of the electrons that were displaced, but instead *doubled* their number. This established that increasing the intensity of light increases current. He also discovered that light below a certain energy threshold would not dislodge any electrons at all.[16]

In 1905, Albert Einstein published his idea that light was *both* a wave and a particle, or rather a wave made up of a stream of small particles: photons. This theory, shown in Figure 2.6, explained the results found by

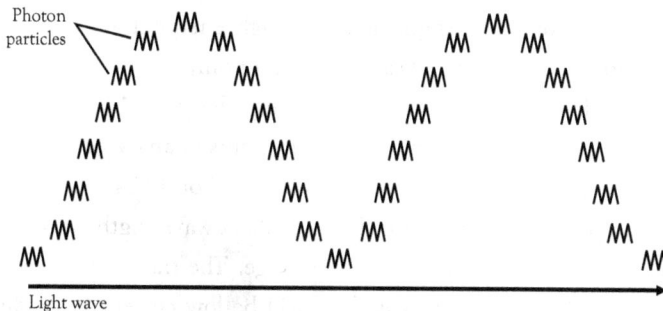

Figure 2.6 Schematic showing the wave-particle nature of light, with light consisting of a wave of photon particles.

Hertz, Thompson and Lenard, and forms the basis of our understanding of light today.

Each photon dislodges one electron from a material, and its resulting kinetic energy is equal to the energy of the photon minus the energy needed to dislodge it. Since one photon dislodges one photoelectron, then light at a higher *intensity* (more photons/second) can dislodge *more* electrons.

- **Voltage (Kinetic energy of the photoelectron) = energy of the photon – energy needed to dislodge photoelectron**
- **Current (Number of photoelectrons) is *proportional* to the intensity of the light.**

We know that power is voltage times current. Current or irradiance is a measure of the amount of sunlight. Voltage depends on the material, specifically the wavelength at which it absorbs light. We call that the *energy bandgap* of the material.

Not all solar radiation is the same. As discussed, we can think of light both as a wave and a particle. It varies in wavelength and its wavelength determines its energy by the relationship **eV (electron Volts) = 1.24/lambda** (lambda is the wavelength in micrometers). This formula for determining a photon's energy is based on German Physicist Max Planck's Equation e (energy of a photon in Joules) = h (a constant) times f (frequency of the light), which relates the energy of a photon (Eph) to several constants, including the speed of light.

Clearly the Eph is highly dependent on that light's frequency, and thus wavelength (lambda)—the higher the frequency the shorter the wavelength. Short wavelength light has high energy. Long wavelength light has low energy. Material can absorb light only at certain parts of the spectrum. Material that absorbs higher energy light has a greater eV. For instance, if the lambda is 1 micrometer, it results in an eV of 1.24, and if the lambda is 10 micrometers, it results in an eV of 0.124.

A material that absorbs light that is of short wavelength absorbs high energy photons and produces a high voltage. The trade-off is that *there is less of that light*, which means there will be low current. In addition, in 1961, a limit of 31 percent photon to photoelectron efficiency was discovered due to any one material's bandgap being unable to absorb the entire EM spectrum. This is known as the "Shockley-Quiesser" limit.

That is why in Figure 2.7, voltage is shown with an arrow pointing to the left. On the other hand, when you have material that absorbs light at longer wavelength, it is lower energy so you have a lower voltage, but you are absorbing more total light.

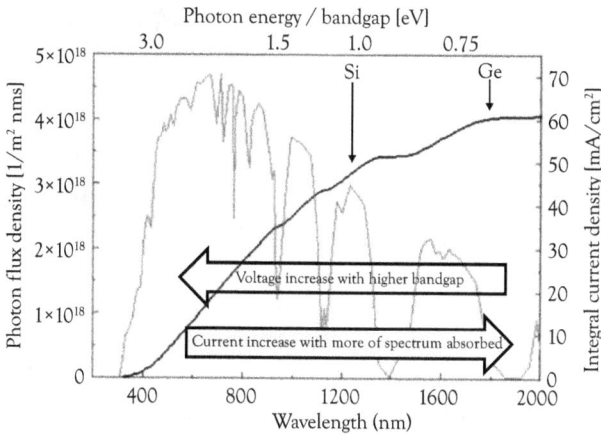

Figure 2.7 How a semiconductor's energy bandgap determines its absorption properties, and thus the voltage and current it can produce.[17]

Notes: On the bottom x axis is the wavelength of the electromagnetic spectrum in nanometers. Its corresponding left y axis is the Photon Flux Density, which is the number of photons per square nanometer per second (the light grey line). It shows that shorter wavelengths have higher photon flux density.

On the top x axis is the photon / energy bandgap of the semiconductor in electronvolts (eV). On its corresponding right y axis is the integral (total) current density in milliamperes per square centimeter, or maximum attainable photocurrent (the black line). It shows that high bandgaps have a low photocurrent, while low bandgaps have a high photocurrent.

This means that high bandgaps absorb a little amount of photon-dense light. Conversely, low bandgaps absorb a high amount of photon-diffuse light. The left and right arrows reinforce this point. Material with a high bandgap absorbs short wavelength light and produces higher voltage (light grey line) but lower current since it absorbs only a small amount of the electromagnetic spectrum (black line).

Conversely, low bandgap and long wavelength means the semiconductor will produce lower voltage but a higher current since it is absorbing more total light from the electromagnetic spectrum but on the whole that light is of lower energy.

No one semiconductor can do it all. Recall that power equals voltage times current, and any one semiconductor has a maximum quantum limit of 31 percent photoelectric conversion efficiency. The arrows pointing to the black line point out two particular semiconductors. Silicon (Si) has a higher bandgap than Germanium (Ge). This means it absorbs less photons than Germanium but they are of higher energy. Cells of diverse materials can be stacked together, called heterojunction solar cells, to take advantage of the different absorption properties of semiconductors to maximize power output. Since Ge absorbs low energy long wavelength light, it would be placed below Si in a heterojunction cell because longer-wavelength photons can penetrate deeper.

Figure 2.8 below shows various materials, their energy bandgaps and their efficiencies. You will notice that regardless of the material none are above 30 percent.

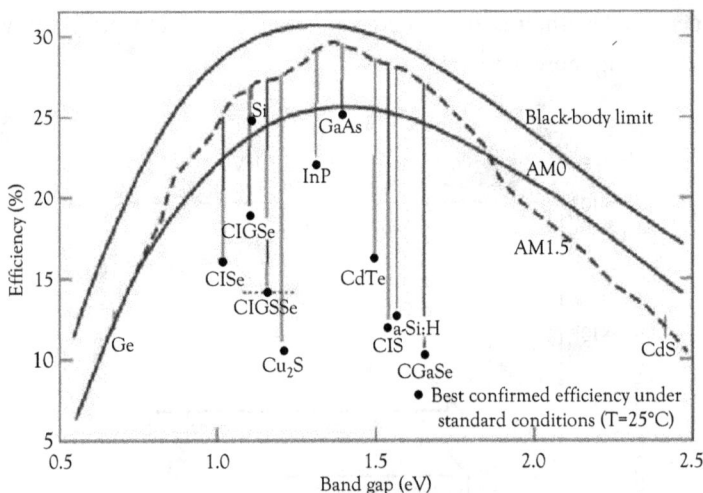

Figure 2.8 Energy bandgaps and efficiencies of various solar cells. The black body limit is the theoretical maximum efficiency. The air mass zero (AM0) is the extraterrestrial irradiance at the top of the atmosphere. The air mass 1.5 (AM1.5) is the terrestrial irradiance used for standard test conditions on the Earth's surface. The AM1.5 has slightly higher efficiency than AM0 due to less infrared and thus heat loss. However, there is more irradiance in space and thus greater output from a space-based PV array compared to a terrestrial array. Note semiconductor efficiencies have increased since the publication of this figure in 1999.[18]

Source: Birkmire, R., and L. Kazmerski. *Harnessing the Sun with Thin-Film Photovoltaics.*

In sum, some materials absorb a little high energy radiation (because photons below a material's energy bandgap are not absorbed) and some absorb a lot of low energy radiation, but photon energy in excess of the material's bandgap is wasted.

Solar Cell Physical Chemistry

The most common material used in PV is *silicon* (Si). The Si atom has 4 valence electrons that form _covalent_, or shared, bonds, making them tightly held by their atoms.

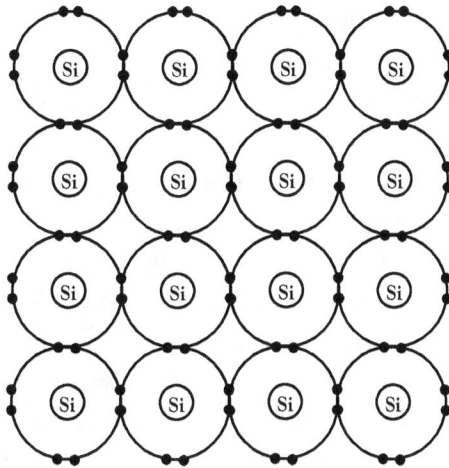

Figure 2.9 Molecular structure of silicon.

When photons strike a Si crystal, the atoms' electrons are too fixed to "jump" to the conduction band. So, we _dope_, or introduce other chemicals, into Si molecules to create imbalances needed to allow electron movement.

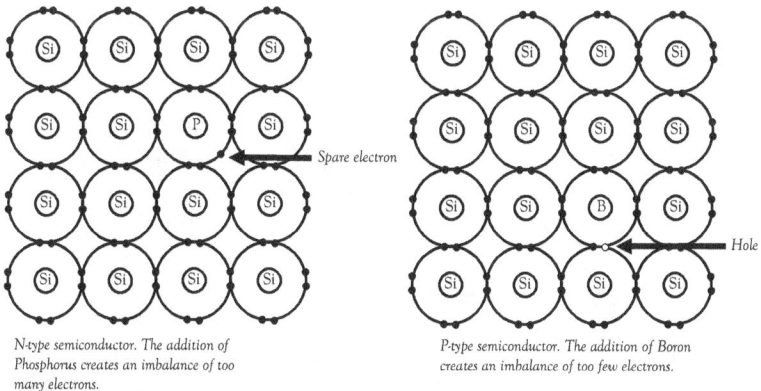

N-type semiconductor. The addition of Phosphorus creates an imbalance of too many electrons.

P-type semiconductor. The addition of Boron creates an imbalance of too few electrons.

Figure 2.10 Molecular structure of P- and N-type semiconductors.

The dopants have different numbers of valence electrons than Si, which has four. Phosphorus (P) has five valence electrons, and is commonly introduced to create the _n-type semiconductor_. Boron (B) has three valence electrons, and is introduced to create the _p-type semiconductor._

Thanks to Phosphorous, the n-type semiconductor has "extra" electrons, which makes it want to get rid of some electrons, and Boron means that the p-type semiconductor has *holes* where electrons could be, making it keen to get hold of new electrons to fill these holes. When an n-type and p-type semiconductor are put together, they form a *p-n junction*.

At the junction, the extra electrons in the n-type are attracted to the positive holes in the p-type, and diffuse into the p-type to fill the holes. As a result, the extra electrons in the p-type give it a negative charge and the "missing" electrons from the n-type lend it a positive charge.

This diffusion of electrons at the junction creates an electric field. Now, when photons reach the p-n junction, the dislodged electrons are attracted to the positively charged n-type semiconductor, and move across the electric field, generating current that can be used in a circuit.*

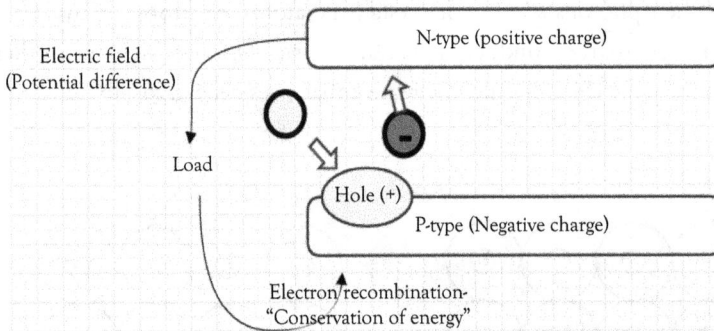

Figure 2.11 Image showing how current is generated at a P-N junction in the presence of a light-source.

Cell Components

Solar cells are made up of many layers. A simplified diagram is shown below. Back and front metallic contacts are needed to complete the

---

* Conductors, such as copper, are not used as PV cells or electronic switching devices, such as transistors, because there is no energy bandgap. The electrons are already moving about freely in the conduction band and thus the requisite electric field with electron-hole pairs cannot be established.

electrical circuit. The n-type semiconductor is sprinkled on top of the p-type. Next comes a contact grid, an antireflective coating to prevent optical loss, and a protective glass cover. p-type Boron is 1,000 times thicker than n-type Phosphorus.

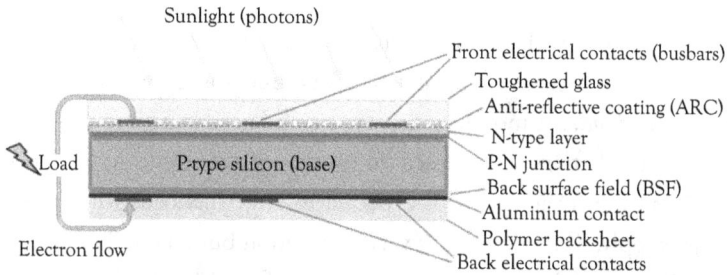

Sunlight (photons)

Front electrical contacts (busbars)
Toughened glass
Anti-reflective coating (ARC)
N-type layer
P-N junction
Back surface field (BSF)
Aluminium contact
Polymer backsheet
Back electrical contacts

Load

P-type silicon (base)

Electron flow

Figure 2.12 Construction of a solar cell including p- and n-type silicon.

Source: Jason Svarc, Clean Energy Reviews[19]

Types of Systems

From a cost of $76/watt for crystalline Si modules in the 1970s to $0.36/watt today, solar energy has come a long way.

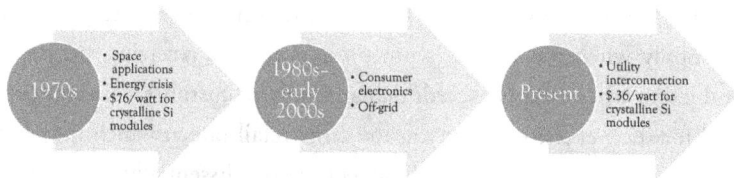

1970s
• Space applications
• Energy crisis
• $76/watt for crystalline Si modules

1980s–early 2000s
• Consumer electronics
• Off-grid

Present
• Utility interconnection
• $.36/watt for crystalline Si modules

Figure 2.13 The development of solar power generation from the 1970s to the present.

There are three major types of solar PV systems:

Type 1: Off-grid, Stand-alone System

The first widely-used type of PV system is the *off-grid, stand-alone system*. It first became popular in the 1970s, adopted by natural living enthusiasts in Northern California. This community, which had been living entirely without electricity or with diesel generators, saw the value in PV and felt the technology was a better reflection of their environmental beliefs than fossil fuels. Their pioneering experiments demonstrated how off-grid households in sunny areas could depend on solar power, leading to the development of the stand-alone systems we see today.

These systems charge a battery that can service the electrical load when demand exceeds the solar system's production. System size is based on *peak demand*, the most electricity you could need in a given day during the year, and battery size is based on the *days of autonomy*, the number of days in a month the battery is expected to serve the loads without solar energy supply. The calculations vary by location but a period of 7 days is generally accepted as a conservative estimate for critical loads, and 2 to 3 days for non-critical loads.[20]

Type 2: Grid-tie System

The *grid-tie* system came of age in the early 1990s, allowing conventional customers to benefit from solar systems while also being connected to the grid. This is now the predominant type of PV installation in the U.S. and Europe. In the *grid-tie* system, customers use solar energy to offset their energy consumption, while remaining connected to the grid.

In this way, the grid effectively acts as the consumer's battery, providing supply when the system is not producing, and receiving the excess production when supply exceeds demand. Often, customers are compensated for their excess electricity at the same retail rate at which they buy electricity in a scheme called *net energy metering*. Essentially, the bidirectional meter runs backward during periods of export, reducing customers' energy bills.

However, the scheme is not globally universal, and many areas are moving toward more complex pricing models as PV installations saturate the grid. Determining system size in this configuration is simple.

System Sizing through Energy Demand: The simplest way to estimate is to take two years of facility energy consumption (kWh). The average annual American household energy consumption is 6,515 kWh. Therefore, average household annual PV system size can be calculated based on the need to meet 6,515 kWh of demand.

Solar irradiation can be considered as fuel. Due to the night, clouds and other obstructions, during a 24-hour day we receive a limited number of hours of "peak sun," defined as 1,000 watts/m². Globally, this ranges from two peak sun hours at the poles to eight peak sun hours close to the equator.

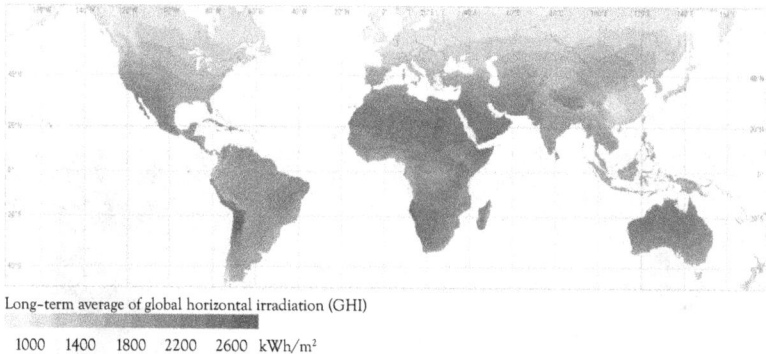

Long-term average of global horizontal irradiation (GHI)

1000   1400   1800   2200   2600   kWh/m²

Figure 2.14 *GHI shown is annual average. To find peak sun hours divide by 365 days.*

Source: © 2019 The World Bank, Solar resource data: Solargis.[21]

The amount of horizontal irradiation that hits a particular area varies according to where it is on the globe, as shown in Figure 2.14. Based on your location, anticipated PV system production can thus be estimated based on PV system size (kW) * number of *peak sun hours (PSH)* * 365 days times * a derating for losses throughout the system (a 15 percent loss is typically used, so we multiply by 85 percent since that is the amount retained).

Annual PV System Production (kWh) = kW System Size * PSH * 365 Days * 0.85 (15 percent Derating)

The kWh produced should equal demand. Given a location and annual household or facility energy consumption, the only missing variable is system size:

PV kW System Size = Annual PV System Production (kWh)/(PSH * 365 days * 0.85)

So, for a location with 6 PSH needing to produce 6,515 kWh, the system size, or capacity, would be 3.5 kW (6,515/(6 * 365 * 0.85).

Solar Array Orientation

Latitude: Latitude impacts the amount of sun available over a given area. At high northern and southern latitudes, there is more air mass through which photons must travel and the radiation is spread over a greater area.

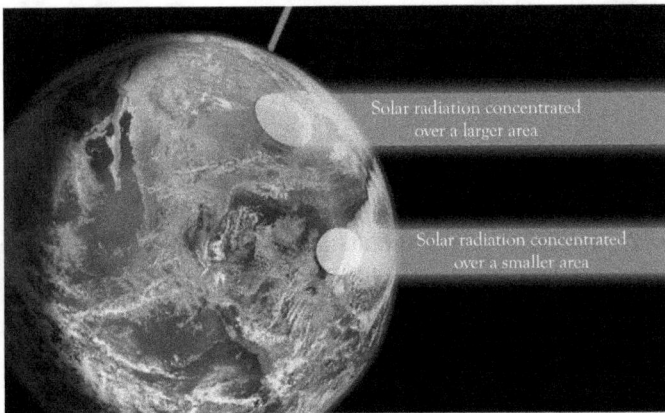

Figure 2.15 The Impact of Latitude on Solar Irradiation.

Source: NASA

As shown in Figure 2.15, at high North and South latitudes, the solar radiation is spread out over a larger area than at the equator. We indicate this by air mass (AM) number. For instance, at AM1, we are at the equator and the sun is directly overhead, perpendicular to us at a 90 degree angle. Solar cells are tested using conditions of AM1.5, approximately the average latitude for the contiguous U.S., because this is where the majority of people live.

The *solar azimuth angle* is the compass direction from which sunlight arrives at a particular site. In the Northern Hemisphere, the sun is predominantly passing by the Earth from the south, while in the Southern Hemisphere the sun is passing by the Earth from the north. This is why modules should be south-facing in the Northern Hemisphere and north-facing in the Southern Hemisphere.

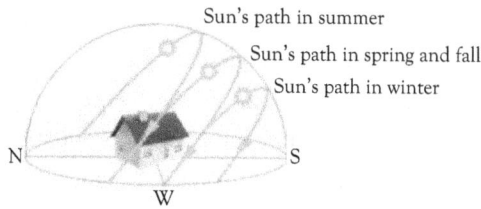

Sun's path in summer

Sun's path in spring and fall

Sun's path in winter

N   S

W

Figure 2.16 The sun's path in the Northern Hemisphere.

Source: Meg Escott. http://www.houseplanshelper.com/floor-plans-for-a-house.html

As the path of the sun varies by location, solar designers use a Solar Pathfinder, or electronic tool to trace the path of the sun during the day in their location. These tools also allow for shade analysis to determine potential sources and impacts of shading.

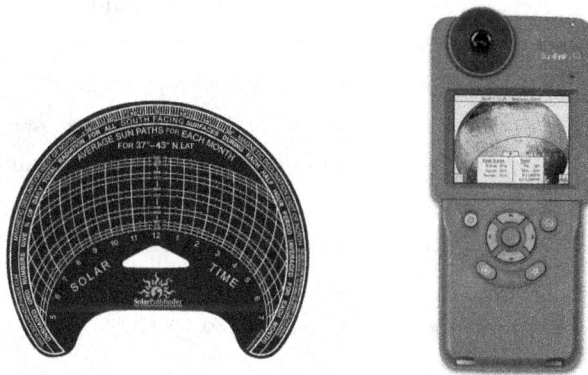

Figure 2.17 Tools for determining a site's solar resource.

Left: Solar Pathfinder for Northern Hemisphere, *Right:* Solmetric Suneye

Tilt: The tilt angle is the angle between the PV module and the sun. Clearly, we want the most concentrated light to hit our solar array. The most concentrated light is perpendicular to us. If we were at the equator, the optimal tilt would be 0 degrees, no tilt, or flat. The farther from the equator, the more the module should be tilted toward the equator. Thus, the module should be tilted at an angle equal to the latitude of the site, called *latitude tilt*.

For annual production, latitude tilt, or tilted down from horizontal by an angle equal to the latitude of the site, is ideal because on average throughout the year the modules will collect the most sunlight at this angle. Again, the modules will produce the most power if the sun strikes them at a perfectly perpendicular angle.

As shown in Figure 2.16, during the summer, the sun is high in the sky so if you want to optimize just for summer production the modules would be tilted at latitude minus 15 degrees. During the winter, the sun is low in the sky so the tilt angle optimized for winter production would be latitude plus 15 degrees.

The use of trackers, particularly dual-axis with two motors that change the tilt angle and compass direction, maximizes solar collection.

Module Number Through Coldest Temperature for String Inverters

The second level of analysis is selecting the optimal number of modules. Although many newer PV systems have microinverters connected to one or two modules, traditional arrays use *string inverters* that collect the output of a certain number of modules wired in series. The maximum number of modules that can be wired in series is based on the maximum input voltage of the inverter. Recall from Chapter 1 that in a series circuit the total voltage is the sum of the individual voltages. When solar modules are wired in series, from the positive terminal of one module to the negative terminal of the subsequent module and so on, the total voltage is the sum of the individual modules.

Figure 2.18 shows three strings of 10 modules each. The modules in each string are wired in series to increase the voltage—from the negative terminal of one module to the positive terminal of the next. The strings are wired in parallel—the positive terminal of the first module in each string is connected in the combiner box. Wiring strings in parallel increases the current, as explained in Chapter 1. The total current of the array will be 14.85 amps (4.95 amps * 3).

Voltage is sensitive to temperature. The lower the temperature the higher the voltage (think of electrons tightly packed due to the cold). Also, open circuit voltage is higher than maximum power voltage (in an open circuit the electrons are not flowing and there is no *voltage drop*). On the other hand, the higher the temperature the lower the voltage.

Combiner Box Wiring

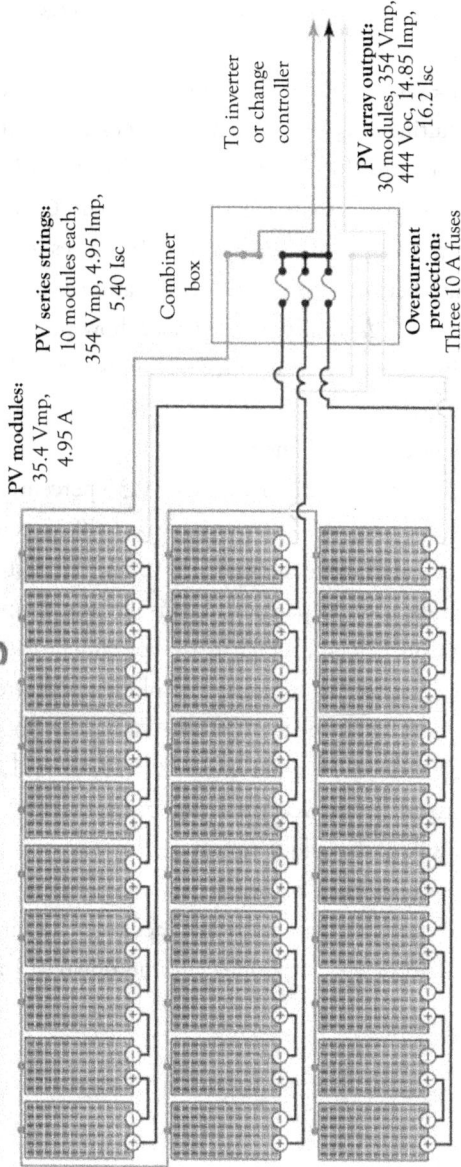

PV modules:
35.4 Vmp,
4.95 A

PV series strings:
10 modules each,
354 Vmp, 4.95 Imp,
5.40 Isc

Combiner
box

To inverter
or change
controller

PV array output:
30 modules, 354 Vmp,
444 Voc, 14.85 Imp,
16.2 Isc

Overcurrent
protection:
Three 10 A fuses

Figure 2.18 Diagram showing solar modules wired in series in a string and strings in parallel.

Source: https://www.homepower.com/home

Therefore, PV designers size a system based on the maximum string inverter input voltage in cold weather. If that voltage is exceeded, the inverter is shut off. Designers must also consider the minimum string inverter input voltage in warm weather. If that voltage is *not* met, the inverter does not turn on.

Let's take an example for maximum modules in a string in cold weather: By consulting NOAA weather data, let's say we find the coldest expected temperature in our climate over 50+ years is –11 degrees Celsius. Module voltage is based on *Standard Test Conditions (STC)*, which is a temperature of 25 degrees Celsius. This gives us a difference of –36 degrees Celsius between the coldest temperature and STC (–11–25). The module specifies a *Temperature Coefficient,* how much the open circuit voltage will increase or decrease with the temperature. In the module in Figure 2.19 below, it is –0.33 percent/C (note Kelvin and Celsius can be used interchangeably for changes). This means that for every degree higher than the STC the Voc will decrease by 0.33 percent, and for every degree lower than the STC the Voc will increase by 0.33 percent.

Multiplying the difference between STC and coldest temperature (–36 degrees Celsius * –0.33 percent/Celsius) by the temperature coefficient gives us 11.88 percent, which is by how much the open circuit voltage (Voc) will increase as a result of the cold temperature.

The Figure 2.19 module Voc is 37.5v. The increase in Voc is 11.88 percent, which is 1.1188 or 1.12 times greater than 37.5v (11.88/100 + 1). Multiply 1.12 times 37.5v and you get 42 Voc as the highest Voc that could be expected as a result of the cold temperature.

If the string inverter has a maximum voltage of 600v, then the maximum number of modules that could be placed on this circuit in series is simply 600v/42 Voc = 14.29 modules. Round down to 14 modules.*

---

* See Sean White's "Solar Photovoltaic Basics: A Study Guide for the NABCEP Entry Level Exam" for more examples.

Cold Temperature String Sizing

Cold expected temperature = –11 C

Difference Between Coldest Temperature & 25 C Standard Test Conditions (STC) = (–11 – 25) = –36

Temperature Coefficient Voc (open circuit voltage) = –36 C * –0.33 percent/Celsius (from module specifications) = 11.88 percent increase Voc

Voc of Module = 37.5V

Increase in Voc cold = 11.88/100+1 = 1.12 * 37.5 V = 42 Voc

Max Input Voltage of Inverter = 600v

Max Number of Modules in Series = 600v/42 Voc cold = 14.29 modules

ROUND DOWN = 14 modules

bOVIET

60 Cell Poly 250-270W

BVM6610P

High Quality and Reliable Modules Due to Thorough Design and Stringent Quality Control
- Withstand up to 5400 Pa snow load and 2400 Pa wind load
- 1000V DC
- Three times of EL inspection on every cell and module for defect free
- Type 1 fire-rating per UL 1703 edition 3
- High salt and ammonia resistance certified by TUV Rheinland
- 0~+5 W guaranteed positive tolerance on nameplate power output
  Warranty
- 12- year product warranty
- 25-year linear power output warranty
  Comprehensive Certificates for Products and Management
- UL 1703, IEC 61215, IEC 61730, CEC listed, MCS and CE
- ISO 9001 for Quality Management Systems
- ISO 14001 for Environmental Management Systems

Electrical Characteristics STC

	BVM6610P-250	BVM6610P-255	BVM6610P-260	BVM6610P-265	BVM6610P-270
Maximum Power(Pmax)	250W	255W	260W	265W	270W
Maximum Power Current(Imp)	8.31A	8.39A	8.47A	8.52A	8.57A
Maximum Power Voltage(Vmp)	30.1V	30.5V	30.7V	31.2V	31.6V
Short Circuit Current (Isc)	8.85A	8.95A	9.01A	9.20A	9.31A
Open Circuit Voltage (Voc)	37.5V	37.6V	38.0V	38.3V	38.5V
Module Efficiency	15.4%	15.7%	16.0%	16.19%	16.49%
Power Tolerance	0~+5W	0~+5W	0~+5W	0~+5W	0~+5W

STC:AM1.5, Irradiance 1000W/m²,25℃

Thermal Characteristics

Pmax Temperature Coefficient	-0.43%/K
Voc Temperature Coefficient	-0.33%/K
Isc Temperature Coefficient	+0.05%/K
NOCT	113±3.6°F

Figure 2.19 Typical PV module specifications.

Source: Boviet Solar USA.[22]

Strings in Parallel

What arrangement of strings reaps the most power output? In some instances, PV system designers must also take into consideration the inverter's maximum power tracking voltage range and maximum input current to determine the optimal number of strings per inverter.

For instance, if we have a string inverter, such as the SMA Sunny Boy in Figure 2.20, with a maximum power tracking voltage of 220v to 480v and a maximum current of 15 amps, and the Voc of our modules is 48.3v, we would find that the optimal design window would be between 10 modules (480v/48.3 Voc = 9.9, round up) and 6 modules (220v/48.3 Voc = 5.5), round up.

SMA Sunny Boy
2500HF-US >

INPUT (DC)

Recommended PV Power (STC)	3125 W
Max Voltage	600 V
Peak Power Tracking Voltage	220 V - 480 V
Min Start Voltage	220 V
Max Current	15 A (per channel)

OUTPUT (AC)

Maximum Output Power	2500 W
Nominal AC Voltage	208 V / 240 V
Voltage Range	183 - 229 V / 211 - 264 V
Frequency	60.0 Hz
Max Current	12.0 A / 10.4 A

DOCUMENTATION

Data Sheet	SMA SunnyBoy HF
Manual	SMA SunnyBoy HF
Warranty	SMA Solar

Figure 2.20 Sample inverter specifications.

Source: SMA Sunny Boy 2500 HF-US[23]

If our module short circuit current is 5.8 amps, we can wire two strings in parallel per inverter and be below the inverter's allowable 15 amps input (5.8 amps * 2 strings in parallel * 1.25 maximum circuit current* = 14.5 amps < 15 amps).

If our inverter has a maximum power capacity of 3,125 watts, and each module is 215 watts, we can have two strings of 7 modules (8 modules would be too many as 8 * 215 watts * 2 strings = 3,440 watts > 3,215 watts). Whereas, with 7 modules we would get 3,010 watts per inverter (7 modules * 215 watts * 2 strings = 3,010 watts < 3,125 watts). Or, we could have one string of 10 modules, but that would only get us 2,150 watts per inverter.

Clearly, two strings of 7 modules wired in parallel per inverter would maximize the power output of our array.

Type 3: Grid-tie battery backup system

The primary drawback of a grid-tie system is that during a grid outage, *anti-islanding* protections on the inverter automatically shut off the system to protect utility maintenance workers, which takes us to the third system. The third type of system, *grid-tie battery backup*, allows consumers to be connected to the grid *and* have a backup battery to provide power during a power outage.

There are two ways of connecting such a system, DC-coupled and AC-coupled. In a grid-tie DC-coupled system, the PV system charges batteries with a charge controller in DC, and is connected to a *multimode* inverter, which operates in interactive and stand-alone modes. Such an inverter has two outputs, one going to the grid and the other to stand-alone system loads. During a grid power outage, the interactive output of a multimode inverter shuts off, and only stand-alone loads are powered, shown in Figure 2.21.

---

* The National Electrical Code Section 690.8(A)(1)(1), requires that PV system designers use a safety factor of 125 percent of the module or string's short circuit current to determine wire size and compliance with maximum inverter input (or DC) current. This is done because the PV source circuit current is based on solar irradiance and is not controlled by electronics. It is a cautious correction factor as most short circuits are not greater than 7 percent of operating current.

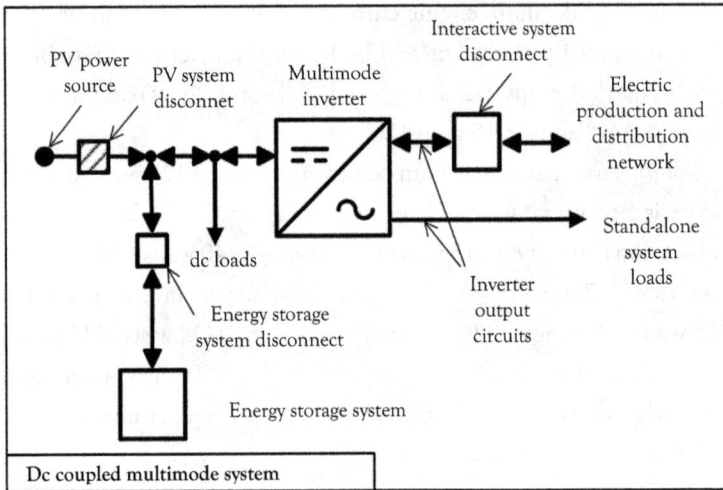

Figure 2.21 DC coupled multimode system.

Source: Figure 690.1(b) of NFPA 70®-2017: National Electrical Code® (NEC®).*

In an AC-coupled system, a PV array is connected to an interactive inverter that supplies stand-alone system loads. Batteries are connected to the facility's electrical network through a multimode inverter that converts excess energy to DC for storage. Thus, in an AC-coupled system, batteries are connected to a PV array on the "AC side."

Although design is more complex in an AC-coupled system, and there is additional cost with two inverters, AC-coupled systems allow more batteries to be easily added and increase independence from the grid since the PV array and batteries could supply the facility's loads simultaneously. AC-coupled systems are becoming increasingly popular due to these additional services, particularly in the context of microgrids. This will be explored more in Chapter 5.

---

* Reproduced with permission from NFPA 70®-2017, National Electrical Code®, Copyright © 2016, National Fire Protection Association, Quincy, MA 02169. This reprinted material is not the complete and official position of the NFPA on the referenced subject, which is represented only by the standard in its entirety which can be obtained through the NFPA web site at www.nfpa.org

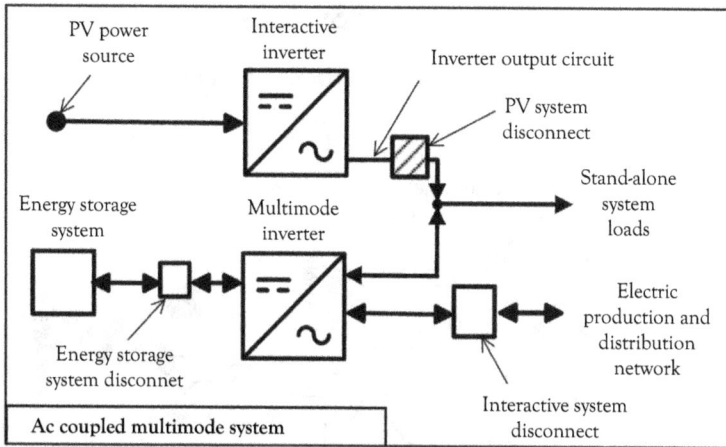

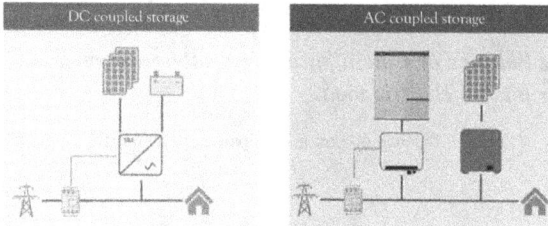

Figure 2.22 AC-coupled multimode system.

Top image is 2017 NEC Figure 690.1(b). Bottom image is from SMA[24]*

Balance of Systems

As discussed, PV arrays require a network of additional components known as the *Balance of Systems* or *BoS*.

PV modules (or other   Charge
renewable energy source)   controller

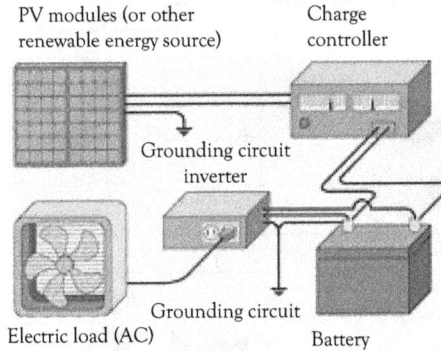

Grounding circuit
inverter

Grounding circuit
Electric load (AC)   Battery

Figure 2.23 Simple balance of system for a stand-alone system requiring AC power for the electric load.

Source: U.S. Department of Energy. Balance-of-System Equipment Required for Renewable Energy Systems. [25]

The Balance of System needs to safely perform three functions:

1. *Condition the energy*: convert the DC power generated into AC power for consumption by common AC equipment.
2. *Transmit the energy*: conduct the AC electricity to the electrical load(s).
3. *Store the energy*: either charge a battery for future use, or transmit the energy to the grid for storage.

Although the specific equipment will vary by the customers' needs, the key equipment in most systems is as follows:

Function	Equipment	Use	Type of PV system
Conditioning the energy	Inverters (convert DC to AC)	The DC electricity generated by the PV system is converted to AC for use by conventional electrical loads Also, inverters condition electricity to match the quality requirements of the load or the electric grid: voltage, phase, frequency, and sine wave. In addition, they output electricity from the solar array at its maximum voltage and current, called the *maximum power point (MPP)*	All except for some off grid stand-alone systems, primarily in the developing world
	Charge controller	Regulate the current from the PV system to the battery to ensure the battery does not become over-charged or over-drained	Stand-alone and grid-tie battery backup systems
Transmitting the energy	Wiring	Conducts the generated current from the PV system to the rest of the Balance of System and the load. Also includes grounding for protection	All
Storing the energy	Battery	Stores power generated by the PV system	Stand-alone and grid-tie battery backup systems
Monitoring the energy	Software, meters and instrumentation	Monitors battery state of charge, energy consumption and/or power sent to and drawn from the grid	All
Safety equipment	Safety disconnects (AC and DC circuit breakers); Grounding Equipment; Surge protection	Protects people, PV system, and other equipment from short circuits	All

Wind Turbines

History of Wind Energy

Wind energy has been used for natural ventilation, sail power, and even prayer wheels for thousands of years. By the 1800s, household and industrial windmills were used across Europe and North America to power mechanical loads from wells and water pumps to saw and grain mills.

USA		Europe
Windmills pump water and wind turbines generate electricity for rural homes and businesses Wind power showcased at 1893 Chicago World's Fair	1890s	
	1910s	72 small wind-powered generators built across Denmark
1927: Jacobs Wind opens in Minneapolis, which will go on to produce 30,000 small wind turbines for small farms outside areas covered by the grid	1920s	
Only 10 percent of farms are served by the grid. Instead, farms and small infrastructure use wind turbines to generate electricity 1931: The Darrieus wind turbine is invented, which can use wind power from any direction. It is a type of vertical axis wind turbine whereby the rotor is transverse, or along, the wind	1930s	Large wind turbine used in Balaklava in the former USSR from 1931 to 1942
1941: World's first megawatt-size wind Turbine in Vermont feeds electricity to the grid during WWII	1940s	During WWII, German submarines used small wind-powered generators to charge the submarine batteries
Gas prices soar, leading to increased interest and research into wind power, including by NASA, and a return to some of the small wind generators used in the 1930s 1978: Public Utilities Regulatory Policies Act "requires utilities to buy a certain amount of electricity from renewable energy sources, including wind"	1970s	1978: Students and teachers at the Tvind school in Denmark construct the world's first multi-megawatt wind turbine Danish blade supplier Okaer changes the dominant rotation of wind turbines from counter-clockwise (like windmills) to clockwise

Large wind farms in California, lead to discoveries of the environmental impacts of wind turbines and the importance of location	1980s	European machinery manufacturers send hundreds of wind turbines to California 1982: European Wind Energy Association (EWEA) forms in Stockholm, Sweden 1982: Europe's first wind farm opens in Greece 1988: UK plans first wind farm
1992: Energy Policy Act provides a 1.5 cents/kWh tax credit for wind power generated electricity 1993: National Wind Technology Center built	1990s	1990: Europe's largest wind farm opens in Denmark 1991: EWEA launches action plan for the development of European wind energy, with a target of 100,000 MW of capacity by 2013 1995: European wind energy production exceeds that of the United States
2008: US wind power capacity reaches 25.4 GW	2000s	2000: First large-scale offshore wind farm opens in Denmark 2005: Global Wind Energy Council formed, with members from over 50 countries 2009: Wind generation provides 2 percent of global energy
2012: US wind power capacity reaches 60 GW, or 15 million homes worth of power 2013: First US offshore turbine connected to grid 2018: US wind power capacity reaches 89 GW, or 20 million homes worth of power	2010s	2010: Over 20 percent of Danish energy now produced by wind 2011: World's second floating offshore multi-megawatt turbine installed off Portuguese coast 2012: World's largest offshore wind farm opens off the coast of the UK 2016: China now has more cumulative wind installations than the EU

It was not until 1887, however, that wind power was used to generate electricity. The first known wind turbine (as opposed to windmill, which is used to pump water) was constructed by Professor James Blyth in Marykirk, Scotland in July 1887, using a 10 meter tall cloth-sailed wind turbine to generate electricity for his holiday cottage. That winter, Charles F. Brush constructed a much larger wind turbine in Cleveland, Ohio, which generated electricity for his laboratory until power stations began to electrify the city in 1900. In 1891, Poul la Cour constructed a small wind turbine to generate electricity for a high school in Askov, Denmark, and, by 1895, used the turbine to light the whole village.

Since then, wind energy production has evolved synergistically on both sides of the Atlantic, generating the distinctive wind farms that we recognize in our landscapes today.[26,27]

How Do Wind Turbines Work?

Similar to a conventional generator, wind turbines take advantage of a prime mover, wind, to spin a shaft that converts mechanical to electrical energy.

A wind turbine is made up of a *rotor*, moving blades, a *generator* that converts the motion to electricity through induction, a *tail* that changes its direction and protects it in high winds, and a *tower* for optimal height, as shown in Figure 2.24.

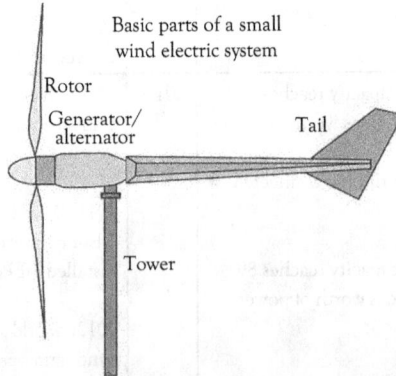

Basic parts of a small
wind electric system

Rotor

Generator/
alternator

Tail

Tower

Figure 2.24 Basic components of a small wind electric system: rotor, generator/alternator, tower, and tail.

Source: Small Wind Guidebook. US Department of Energy.[28]

Harnessing Power from the Wind

Humans have been harnessing the power of the wind for thousands of years, from windmills to ships' sails. Wind is actually another form of solar energy—a product of the uneven heating of the earth's surface. The amount of power a wind turbine can generate is based primarily on the area swept by its rotor. Known as the *swept area*, power is related to the rotor diameter and tells us how much of the wind can be captured—the greater the area, the greater the power.

At low wind speeds a wind turbine will not produce any power because it will not reach the *cut in speed*, typically 8 mph. Too much or inconsistent wind is a bad thing too because wind turbines have a *cut-out speed* at which they shut off to prevent damaging themselves, typically at 55 mph. Also, inconsistent wind speed means intermittent power production, which causes issues for the grid.

Unlike gas or diesel generators, the power output of a wind turbine is primarily based on the swept area captured by the rotor. It is the single

Figure 2.25 *Wind Turbines dot the cliffs of Curacao, an island in the Caribbean. 30 percent of Curacao's energy mix comes from wind turbines. The turbines pictured are each rated at 3.45 MW. Cliffs provide consistent wind-flow.*

most important factor in determining the power output of a wind turbine because power increases exponentially with the swept area.

After rotor diameter, wind speed is crucial to wind energy production. Power is proportional to the cube of wind speed, which means that if you double the velocity, you increase the power eight-fold (i.e., $2^3 = 8$, and $4^3 = 64$).

There are a few steps to estimating the output of a wind turbine. While there are several approaches, the *swept area method* is most commonly used due to the significant impact of swept area on the power output of a wind turbine.

The properties of air affect the energy and power available in the wind. In the swept area method, we first find the *annual power density*, the watts per area of the wind stream intersected by the rotor. In order to find power density, we must know the *kinetic energy* of the wind. The wind's kinetic energy is based on the *mass (m)* of air and its *velocity (v)*. Its mass is based on its *density* and *volume*. Since air is constantly moving, its volume is its velocity times the *area (A)* it passes in a given period of time. Thus:

$$\textbf{Kinetic Energy}\,(\textbf{KE})\,\textbf{of Wind} = \frac{1}{2}\,\text{mv}^2$$

m = mass
v = velocity

Where:

$$\text{m} = \rho\text{Avt}$$

ρ = air density
A = Area
v = velocity
t = time

Substituting the formula for mass into the KE of wind, we get:

$$\textbf{KE of Wind} = \frac{1}{2}\,\rho\text{Atv}^3$$

Since power is energy divided by time, time cancels out and power is thus:

$$\textbf{Power} = \frac{\text{Energy}}{\text{Time}}$$

$$= \frac{1}{2}\rho A v^3$$

Annual Power Density is derived by dividing area from the formula above to get the watts per unit area.

$$\textbf{Annual Power Density}\left(\frac{\textbf{W}}{\textbf{m}^2}\right) = \frac{\text{Power}}{\text{Area}}$$

Thus:

$$\textbf{Annual Power Density} = \frac{1}{2}\rho v^3$$

As you can see, in order to get annual power density, we need air density and velocity. *Air density* varies with pressure, temperature, and humidity. It also increases with decreasing temperature—air is denser in winter than summer, and denser at sea level than at higher elevations.

In order make some estimates of power output, we assume the turbine is at sea-level. This is an acceptable assumption in most locations, unless, of course, you are at very high altitudes and/or in extreme climates. The temperature is 15 degrees Celsius or 288.15 Kelvin (59 degrees F), and the air pressure is 1 standard atmosphere or 101,352.9 Newtons per square meter (N/m²), or 14.7 pounds per square inch.

Air density (ρ) is found by the dividing the *air pressure (P)* in N/m² or Pascal, by the *gas constant (R)*, 287.04 joules per kilogram (J/kg), times *temperature (T)* in *Kelvin (K)*.

$$\textbf{Air Density} = \frac{\text{Air Pressure}}{\left(\text{Gas Constant} * \text{Temperature}\right)}$$

$$\rho = \frac{P}{\left(R * T\right)}$$

Therefore, at sea level, the air density will be:

$$= \frac{101,352.9 \ N/m^2}{\left(287.04 \ J/kg * 288.15 \ K\right)}$$

$$= 1.225 \ kg/m^3 \ (0.07651 lbs/ft^3)$$

In order to find annual power density at sea level we plug air density into our formula for *annual power density*. Again, annual power density is the rate at which energy passes through a unit of area and is given in watts per square meter (W/m²).

$$\textbf{Annual Power Density} = \frac{1}{2} \rho v^3$$

$$\textbf{Annual Power Density at Sea Level} = \frac{1}{2} * 1.225 \frac{kg}{m^3} * v^3$$

$$= 0.6125 \ kg/m^3 * v^3$$

Next, in order to find the rated power output in kW of our wind turbine, we multiply the annual power density times the area swept by the rotor.

$$\textbf{Power} \, (\textbf{kW}) = \frac{\text{Annual Power Density} \left(\frac{W}{m^2}\right) * \text{Swept Area} \left(m^2\right)}{1,000 \, \text{watts} / kW}$$

The swept area is simply the rotor sweeping the area in a circle. Thus, it is the area of a circle (A = πr^2, with r being the radius). If the rotor diameter is 50 meters (164 feet), which is an average utility scale turbine rotor diameter, then:

$$\textbf{Swept Area} \, (\textbf{A}) = \pi * (50/2)^2$$

$$= 1,963 \ m^2$$

In other words, the rotor intercepts 1,963 m² of the wind stream.

We now know the annual power density and the swept area. However, there is one more complication. We can never know for certain the wind speed in the future so the annual power density is based on predictions of wind speed that come from probability distributions. The one we use for calculating probabilities of wind speed is called the *Weibull Distribution*. It is comprised of two parameters and informed by average wind speed *k (shape parameter, dimensionless)* and *C (scale parameter, provides meters/ second units).*

In particular, we use the *Rayleigh Distribution*, a type of Weibull with a k of 2, which is sufficient for most locations in the world, but not areas with very high or low average wind speeds. The Rayleigh lets us use a mean wind speed, but this is not always accurate, as demonstrated by the graphs in Figure 2.26, which show the Rayleigh distribution overestimating actual measured data in Ethiopia.

An *Energy Pattern Factor (EPF)* is used to connect the average speed with the number of hours the wind blows at that speed, which, for a Rayleigh Distribution, is 1.91. We multiply this EPF term by the rest of our terms to calculate annual power density.

Annual Power Density $= 0.6125 \text{ kg/m}^3 * v^3 * \text{EPF}$

v = meters/second (m/s)
EPF = Energy Pattern Factor = 1.91

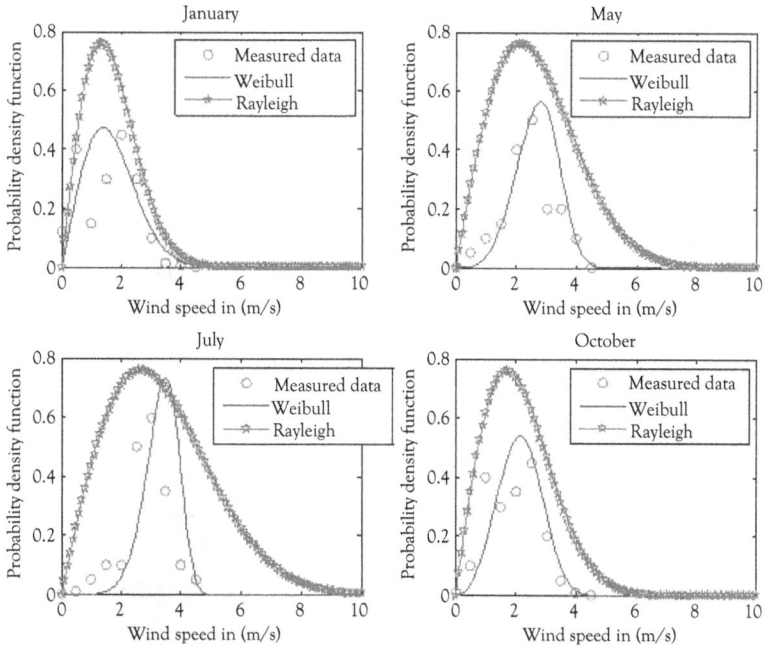

Figure 2.26 How Rayleigh distribution overestimates wind speed.

Source: Nage, American Journal of Modern Energy.[29]

Now, let's say the wind speed is 10 mph at our site, which is 4.47 meters per second. Then,

Annual Power Density = 0.6125 kg/m^3 * 4.47 m/s^3 * 1.91
= **104 W/m^2**

The annual *wind energy density, energy per area (E/A in Wh/m²)* is the amount of energy available to a wind turbine at your site. It is simply the Annual Power Density multiplied by time.

Energy per Area (E/A) = Power Density * 8,760 hours per year

Taking our example above,

E/A = 104 w/m^2 * 8,760 hours per year / 1,000 watts per kW
= **911 kWh/m^2**

We have found that based on an average wind speed of 10 mph the annual amount of energy available to a wind turbine is 911 kWh/m^2. That's a lot of wind!

Figure 2.27 contains a handy table of annual wind power and energy density for the Rayleigh Distribution.

Annual average wind speed		Annual power density	Annual energy density
m/s	mph	W/m^2	kWh/m^2
4	9.0	75	656
5	11.2	146	1,281
6	13.4	253	2,214
7	15.7	401	3,515
8	17.9	599	5,247
9	20.2	853	7,471

Figure 2.27 Annual Wind Power and Energy Density for the Rayleigh distribution.

Courtesy Paul Gipe, Wind Energy for the Rest of Us: A Comprehensive Guide to Wind Power and How to Use It. Bakersfield, California: wind-works.org, 2016. Page 238.

To find the power capacity in kW of our wind turbine, we multiply the Annual Power Density by the Swept Area:

Power (kW) = Annual Power Density (W/m²) × Swept Area (m²)

Recall from our example, for a rotor diameter of 50 meters:

$$\textbf{Swept Area (A)} = \pi * (50/2)^2$$
$$= 1{,}963 \text{ m}^2$$

Thus, for a wind speed of 4.47 meters per second (10 mph), and a rotor diameter of 50 meters, an average utility-scale turbine, we see that the wind turbine power output is:

$$\textbf{Power (kW)} = 104 \text{ W/m}^2 * 1{,}963 \text{ m}^2$$
$$= 204{,}152 \text{ watts}/1{,}000 \text{ watts/kW}$$
$$= \textbf{204 kW}$$

Convert that capacity to annual energy (204 kW * 8,760 hours/year) and you get 1,787 MWh per year.

However, the **Annual Energy Output** must be derated because of the *Betz Limit*, which states that wind turbines can deliver, at most, 59.3 percent of the power in the wind available to the rotor. A wind turbine simply cannot capture all of the power available because they work by slowing down passing wind to extract energy. If 100 percent of the energy was extracted then all of the wind would have to stop, preventing additional air from entering, and halting the turbine. In reality, most turbines achieve 20 to 30 percent efficiency due to kinetic to electrical conversion losses and changes in wind speed and direction.*

Therefore, after derating, and assuming a conservative 20 percent efficiency, we could expect our turbine to produce 357 MWh of energy per year (1,787 MWh * 0.2). To determine if the wind turbine makes economic sense we can calculate payback and return on investment.

Let's take an example:
You are a developer with a turbine that produces 357 MWh/year and have a PPA with the utility for your energy of $110 per MWh. How long will it take to pay off the machine? What is the return on investment? Assume the total installed cost was $750,000.

---

* Downtime for maintenance is also included in this conversion efficiency loss.

To calculate annual revenue, we multiply 357 MWh times $110 per MWh to get $39,270.

Payback (years) = Total Cost / Annual Revenue
$750,000/$39,270
= 19 years

Return on Investment (ROI) = Annual Revenue / Total Cost
$39,270/$750,000 = 0.05 * 100
= 5 percent

The revenue from your investment will be paid back in 19 years and you will receive a 5 percent return. Note this is a simple payback period as it does not account for interest and inflation. Accounting for the *time value of money*, or changes to money over time, will be discussed in Chapter 3.

Summary

Calculating the output of a wind energy turbine is complex. Unlike fossil fuel generators, the generator size has little to do with the power output of a wind turbine. Estimating energy output of a wind turbine involves determining the power in the wind, and then the amount of that power captured by the wind turbine. With that information, we can calculate the economics of an investment in a wind turbine.

To recap, to estimate the energy output of our utility-scale wind turbine with a 50 meter diameter rotor and an average annual wind speed of 4.47 meters/second:

Step 1: Find the *power* density of the wind at a particular site. We assume sea level conditions and a Rayleigh Distribution.

Power (kW) = Annual Power Density (W/m²) * Swept Area (m²)
$$= 104 \text{ W/m}^2 * 1,963 \text{ m}^2$$
$$= 204,152 \text{ watts}/1,000 \text{ watts}/ \text{ kW}$$
$$= 204 \text{ kW}$$

Step 2: Find the *energy* passing through the rotor in one year.

Energy (kWh) = Power (kW) * Time (hours)
$$= 204 \text{ kW} * 8760 \text{ hours } (1 \text{ year} = 8,760 \text{ hours})$$
$$= 1,787,040/1,000 \text{ kW/MW}$$
$$= 1,787 \text{ MWh/year}$$

Step 3: De-rate for Betz Limit, conversion losses, and efficiency.

Annual Estimated Output (AEO) = kWh * Overall Conversion Efficiency
$$= 1787 \text{ MWh/year} * 0.20$$
$$= 357 \text{ MWh/year}$$

Electrochemical Systems: The Hydrogen Fuel Cell and Batteries

Energy storage is critical to enabling large amounts of solar and wind on the grid. While hydrogen and batteries get the most attention, it may come as a surprise that the majority of grid-scale energy storage today comes from *pumped hydropower*, which is storing water by pumping it up to a reservoir during periods of excess supply, and then reversing the pump during periods of high demand to spin a turbine and generate electricity.

Pumped hydro, however, is of finite supply and globally we have used many of these natural resources. Electrochemical energy storage solutions are urgently needed to mitigate variable supply, and are thus critical to a renewable energy future. Two parallel trends are emerging to meet this challenge: the use of hydrogen to power fuel cells and for industrial processes, and batteries.

Hydrogen Fuel Cell: Fuel cells represent an attractive option for residential power and vehicles. The most common commercial fuel cell is the *Proton Exchange Membrane* (PEM). As shown in Figure 2.28 below, it works through bringing neutral hydrogen gas into an *anode*, an electrode

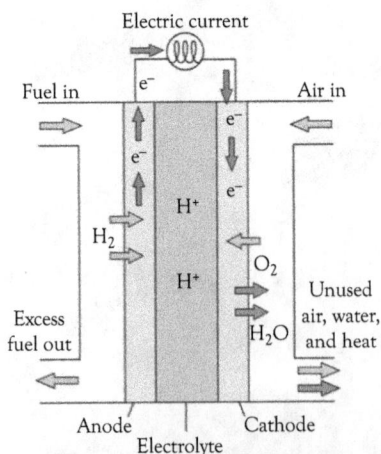

Figure 2.28 A single cell of the PEM fuel cell. The PEM membrane was developed by the Dupont Company.

Source: Wikimedia Commons.[30]

in an electrochemical cell where *oxidation* occurs, or an element's (hydrogen) electrons are lost. The anode in a PEM is comprised of platinum on carbon. The lost electrons can be put to work in a circuit to power loads, and then return to the <u>*cathode*</u>, the electrode where *reduction* occurs, or an element, in this case oxygen, gains electrons. Oxygen from air is supplied to the cathode, which is comprised of platinum on carbon graphite. The oxygen takes the electrons that returned in the reduction reaction, and the hydrogen *protons*, positive ions, which have migrated down through the PEM, to produce water as a byproduct.

The hydrogen input required can be generated by *electrolysis*, a technique using a DC voltage to separate the hydrogen from oxygen in water. Since this process is not naturally occurring, it requires a lot of energy, but this can be provided by hydro, solar or wind power. It operates at about 70 degrees Celsius, and, as such, is suitable for use in residences and cars. In addition to fuel cell-powered <u>*combined heat and power*</u> (CHP) systems for homes and vehicles, hydrogen can be compressed, stored, and transported for use in industrial processes. Thus, it is envisioned that fuel cells are a critical component of a future *Hydrogen Economy*, transforming both the electric grid and transportation sector.

Since there are no mechanical steps involved in the fuel cell, it is possible to achieve 50 percent efficiency for vehicles as compared to 20 to 25 percent efficiency for gas-powered vehicles. Also, since waste heat is put to use in CHP, these systems achieve 80 percent efficiency, as compared to 40 to 55 percent efficiency from a conventional power plant. Hydrogen produced by renewable energy, as opposed to natural gas steam reforming, produces zero CO_2 emissions, with only water is the byproduct.

Current limitations include a large energy requirement needed to compress the gas, lack of an existing infrastructure for hydrogen transport and storage, flammability, and insufficient renewable energy for hydrogen production. However, as solar PV continues its steep cost decline, it could be feasible to use excess solar for hydrogen production through electrolysis.

Batteries: Batteries represent an alternative electrochemical energy storage solution that has been more rapidly commercialized than fuel cells. In a battery that is providing power, the *cathode* is considered the positive terminal while the *anode* is the negative terminal. As discussed in Chapter 1, the first battery was created in 1800 by Alessandro Volta. His battery, known as a "Voltaic Pile," stacked together discs of zinc and copper, separated by blotting paper soaked in brine. The zinc was *oxidized* (losing electrons) with the water in the blotting paper. Each atom of zinc lost two electrons, which were then free to move as current through a circuit.

Diverse battery technologies can be compared using several criteria, including cost, lifespan, *depth of discharge (DoD)*, *roundtrip efficiency*, and *energy density*. DoD is the maximum percentage of a battery's capacity that should be used, beyond which the battery's life will be shortened. A battery with a high DoD means that one can use most of its capacity, while a battery with a low DoD means it has limited useful capacity. A good DoD would be 95 percent and more. Completely depleting a battery is not advised as it severely reduces its lifespan.

Roundtrip efficiency is simply the energy output from a battery divided by the energy input to charge the battery. Energy density is defined as the amount of energy stored in a given volume or mass. Since a PV system is rated for at least 25 years, it is highly advised to use a battery with a high DoD, roundtrip efficiency, and energy density, and with low maintenance costs. It is especially important to select a battery with a high DoD for PV and wind systems because there will not always be enough energy to fully charge the battery due to intermittent supply. For that reason, one should not use lead acid batteries for PV and wind systems, despite their low upfront cost.

Table 2.1 provides an overview of three major battery technologies and their performance along these parameters.

Table 2.1 Primary battery technologies

Battery technology	Operation	Uses	Advantages	Disadvantages
Lead acid	Charge and discharge of sulfuric acid between positive and negative plates (electrodes).	Vehicles, portable equipment	Low upfront cost, mature technology, roundtrip efficiency of 80 percent	Short life, low depth of discharge, low energy density, sulfation on terminals due to depletion of charge increases

	On the positive plate the electrolyte of concentrated sulfuric acid stores most of the chemical energy. On the negative plate sulfate ions are repelled and hydrogen ions attracted			maintenance cost and reduces life. Lack of charge from solar and wind can lead to sulfation and reduce life.
Lithium ion	Lithium ions transferred between electrodes	Consumer electronics, large-scale energy storage, solar plus storage, microgrids	Light and high energy density, high depth of discharge (some have 100 percent)	High upfront cost. Roundtrip efficiency of 70–80 percent. Lose charge over time. Heat up and ignite at high temperatures.
Flow battery	Electrolytes stored in two separate tanks are pumped past a membrane	Large-scale energy storage	High depth of discharge (some have 100 percent), low maintenance. Long life	High upfront cost. Low energy density (a lot of space required)

Fuel Cells vs. Batteries

The debate over hydrogen fuel cells and batteries is contentious, particularly in the transportation sector. The solutions represent divergent technological pathways and R&D priorities in a constrained funding environment. In 2014, Elon Musk, CEO of electric vehicle (EV) firm Tesla Motors and SpaceX called hydrogen vehicles "mind-boggingly stupid."[31] On the other hand, Japan is putting its money on hydrogen, planning to become the world's first hydrogen society with 160 hydrogen stations and 40,000 fuel cell vehicles by March 2021.[32]

While currently more expensive than EVs, a hydrogen fuel cell vehicle can be refueled in under 5 minutes, as compared to 30 minutes to 8 hours for EVs, depending on the type of charging station. While a transition to either electrochemical energy storage system will require more R&D, both energy sources will likely play a role in a future dominated by renewable energy.

Chapter 2 Questions

1. A river has an average flow of 55 m³/s. At Location 1, a natural waterfall provides 10 meters of head. At Location 2, a proposed dam could provide 20 meters of head. What is the power, in MW, produced at each location? Which is the better location?
2. Define two methods for measuring flow.
3. What is the impact of a material's energy bandgap (eV) on its absorption properties and the voltage and current it can provide? What is the Shockley-Quiesser limit?
4. Determine the maximum number of modules per string that can be placed on a string inverter with the following specifications:
   - STC = 25 C. Module Voc = 36v.
   - Coldest expected temperature = –20 C.
   - Temperature coefficient Voc = –.33 percent/C.
   - Maximum input voltage of inverter = 500V.
5. Estimate the Annual Energy Output of a wind turbine with a 10 meter radius and an average wind speed of 5 m/s. Assume sea level conditions, Rayleigh distribution and overall conversion efficiency of 20 percent.
6. For the wind turbine in question 5, determine the payback period in years and return on investment. Assume an installed cost of $125,000 and that you will sell the energy to the utility for 10 cents per kWh. Is it worth the investment to you?
7. Compare and contrast the chemistry and economics of the hydrogen fuel cell and one type of battery using the information above and your own research. Which do you think will have a greater impact on the future of energy storage? Explain.

Chapter 2 Glossary

Anode: electrode in an electrochemical cell where an element's electrons are lost (oxidation occurs). In a battery sending power, the anode is the negative terminal.

Cathode: an electrode in an electrochemical where an element gains electrons (reduction occurs). In a battery supplying power, the cathode is the positive terminal.

Combined Heat and Power (CHP): Generating electricity while capturing usable heat in the same process. Results in greater efficiencies.

Conduction band: an area inside a crystal structure containing delocalized electrons that can move freely and conduct current.

Covalent: A type of chemical bond where electrons are shared between two adjacent atoms, so they are not free to move as current.

Depth of Discharge (DoD): The maximum percentage of a battery's capacity that should be used, beyond which the battery's life will be shortened.

Doping: Introducing other chemicals into a silicon and other semiconductor's crystal structure to allow for better flow of electrons in its unreacted state, or otherwise alter its electrical, optical and structural properties.

Energy density: The amount of energy stored in a given volume or mass.

Non-renewable energy: Energy resources that cannot be renewed or replenished on a human time scale. Examples include fossil fuels such as oil, gas, and coal.

N-type semiconductor: A semiconductor formed from Silicon doped with Phosphorus.

Photon: Particles of light or electromagnetic radiation.

P-N junction: The interface between p- and n-type semiconductors, resulting in an electric field.

P-type semiconductor: A semiconductor formed from Silicon doped with Boron.

Pumped hydropower: energy storage by pumping water up to a reservoir during periods of excess supply, and then reversing the pump during periods of high demand to generate electricity through a turbine.

Renewable energy: Energy resources that can be renewed or replenished on a human time scale. Examples include hydropower, solar power, wind power, geothermal, and biofuels.

Roundtrip efficiency: Energy output from a battery divided by the energy input to charge the battery.

Semiconductor: a substance that can conduct more current than an insulator (e.g., plastic) but less than a conductor (e.g., copper). Silicon is perhaps the best-known semiconductor.

Valence shell: the outer shell of electrons in an atom.

Voltaic: related to the production of electricity.

References

1. PBS. n.d. https://pbs.org/tesla/ll/ll_niagara.html (accessed September 15, 2018).
2. Yongli. December 02, 2015. "Smuggler-Union Hydroelectric Power Plant." *Articles|Colorado Encyclopedia*, https://coloradoencyclopedia.org/article/smuggler-union-hydroelectric-power-plant (accessed September 25, 2018).
3. "U.S. Energy Information Administration—EIA—Independent Statistics and Analysis." *Factors Affecting Gasoline Prices—Energy Explained, Your Guide To Understanding Energy—Energy Information Administration*, https://eia.gov/electricity/monthly/epm_table_grapher.php?t=epmt_6_07_b (accessed September 15, 2018).
4. To learn more, check out "Measuring Flow Rate with Weirs" https://youtube.com/watch?v=t3iEo7zjR60&t=107s
5. "How to Measure Water Flow of Water Site for a Micro Hydro Power Plant?" *Suneco Hydro*, September 03, 2018. https://micro-hydro-power.com/how-to-measure-water-flow.htm (accessed September 15, 2018).
6. Tennessee Valley Authority. August 18, 2000. https://commons.wikimedia.org/wiki/File:Hydroelectric_dam.svg
7. Bonsor, K. June 28, 2018. "How Hydropower Plants Work." *How Stuff Works Science*, https://science.howstuffworks.com/environmental/energy/hydropower-plant1.htm (accessed September 15, 2018).
8. CCEP Fact Sheet. n.d. *Technical paper*, https://usaid.gov/sites/default/files/documents/1862/CCEP_FactSheet_040317.pdf (accessed September 15, 2018).
9. Ginsberg, M. 2018. "Personal Video of CCEP Micro-hydropower Plant." https://facebook.com/mginsberg/videos/10101482600403775/ (accessed September 15, 2018).

10. Perlman, Howard, and USGS. n.d. "Three Gorges Dam: The World's Largest Hydroelectric Plant." *Three Gorges Dam: World's Biggest Hydroelectric Facility*, https://water.usgs.gov/edu/hybiggest.html (accessed August 28, 2018).

11. About TGP. n.d. "China Three Gorges Corporation." http://ctgpc.com/english/index.html (accessed December 29, 2017).

12. Hays, J. n.d. "Yangtze River." *Facts and Details*. http://factsanddetails.com/china/cat15/sub99/item460.html (accessed October 21, 2018).

13. "About TGP." *China Three Gorges Corporation*, http://ctgpc.com/english/index.html (accessed December 29, 2017).

14. "Three Gorges Dam Hydro Electric Power Plant, China." *Power Technology*, https://power-technology.com/projects/gorges/ (accessed August 29, 2018).

15. "Greenhouse Gas Emissions from Dams FAQ." *International Rivers*, https://internationalrivers.org/resources/greenhouse-gas-emissions-from-dams-faq-4064 (accessed October 21, 2018).

16. Stierwalt, S. August 18, 2015. "Einstein's Legacy: The Photoelectric Effect." *Scientific American*, https://scientificamerican.com/article/einstein-s-legacy-the-photoelectric-effect/ (accessed September 15, 2018).

17. Franz-Josef Haug. n.d. "Efficiency Limits of Photovoltaic Energy Conversion." http://www.superstrate.net/pv/limit/

18. Birkmire, R., and L. Kazmerski. 1999. "Harnessing the Sun with Thin-Film Photovoltaics." Institute of Energy Conversion and National Renewable Energy Laboratory, https://www.nrel.gov/docs/fy99osti/29582.pdf

19. Svarc, J. n.d. "Solar PV Cell Construction." *Clean Energy Review*, July 31, 2019. https://cleanenergyreviews.info/blog/solar-pv-cell-construction

20. See online resources for more information on battery and PV sizing for off-grid systems.

21. Global Solar Atlas. n.d. "The World Bank." https://solargis.com/maps-and-gis-data/download/world (accessed January 24, 2017).

22. BVM6610P. "Boviet Solar USA." https://bovietsolarusa.com/wp-content/uploads/2017/01/Boviet_Datasheet_60Cell_Poly_250-270W_BVM6610P_BW.pdf

23. SUNNY BOY 2000HF-US / 2500HF-US / 3000HF-US. "Data Sheet." http://files.sma.de/dl/9524/SB3000HFUS-DEN113412W.pdf

24. "Advantages of AC-coupled high-voltage-battery over alternative solutions?" https://en.sma-jobblog.com/en/advantages-of-ac-coupled-high-voltage-battery-over-alternative-solutions/

25. U.S. Department of Energy. n.d. "Balance-of-System Equipment Required for Renewable Energy Systems." https://energy.gov/energysaver/balance-system-equipment-required-renewable-energy-systems

26. "History of Europe's Wind Industry WindEurope." *WindEurope*, https://windeurope.org/about-wind/history/ (accessed September 15, 2018).

27. Department of Energy. n.d. "History of U.S. Wind Energy." https://energy.gov/eere/wind/history-us-wind-energy (accessed September 15, 2018).

28. Small Wind Guidebook. US Department of Energy. "Office of Energy Efficiency and Renewable Energy." https://windexchange.energy.gov/small-wind-guidebook

29. Nage, G. June 2016. "Analysis of Wind Speed Distribution: Comparative Study of Weibull to Rayleigh Probability Density Function; A Case of Two Sites in Ethiopia." *American Journal of Modern Energy* 2, no. 3, http://article.sciencepublishinggroup.com/html/10.11648.j.ajme.20160203.11.html

30. Proton Exchange Fuel Cell Diagram. https://commons.wikimedia.org/wiki/File:Proton_Exchange_Fuel_Cell_Diagram.svg

31. "Tesla CEO Elon Musk: Hydrogen Fuel Cell Vehicles Are." *Mind-Boggingly Stupid*, January 21, 2014. Retrieved from https://insideevs.com/tesla-ceo-elon-musk-hydrogen-fuel-cell-vehicles-are-mind-boggingly-stupid/

32. "Japan venture aims to build 80 hydrogen fuelling stations by 2022." March 05, 2018. https://reuters.com/article/us-japan-hydrogen/japan-venture-aims-to-build-80-hydrogen-fuelling-stations-by-2022-idUSKBN1GH072

CHAPTER 3

Model 1: Grid-Scale Renewable Energy

Now that we have explored our existing energy system and how renewable energy works, we move into the financial, political, technical and environmental considerations for developing renewable energy projects. In this chapter, we discuss the first "model" of renewable energy production and interconnection—grid-scale. It is a "model" because the financing and interconnection requirements for large-scale projects represent a distinct "regime," or ecosystem of project, different from those at other size scales. In this chapter, the model will be illustrated through two case studies—solar energy in Curacao, and hydropower in Lebanon.

In Chapters 4 and 5, we discuss two additional models—on-site generation, and community-scale/microgrid renewable energy. These chapters will equip the reader with the tools to analyze and implement renewable energy projects of all types.

Renewable energy production model by degree of centralization

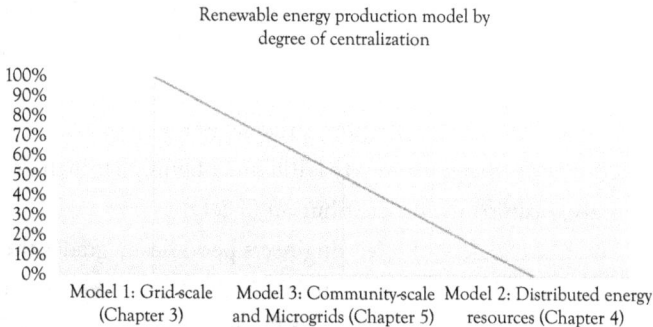

Figure 3.1 Renewable energy production model by degree of centralization. The more centralized the farther from the end user. Grid-scale systems are the most traditional centralized systems that send power over great distances to customers. Community-scale and microgrids are closer to users, and distributed energy resources are at the site of consumption.

Investment in Infrastructure: Competing for Coveted Capital

There is a significant global demand for infrastructure investment. According to the McKinsey Global Institute, $57 Trillion in infrastructure investment, or 3.5 percent of global Gross Domestic Product (GDP), will be needed by 2030, 21 percent of which will be for power.[1]

Based on projections of demand by infrastructure segment,
about $57 trillion, or 3.5 percent of global GDP, is needed through 2030
Global investment, 2013-30
$ trillion, constant 2010 dollars

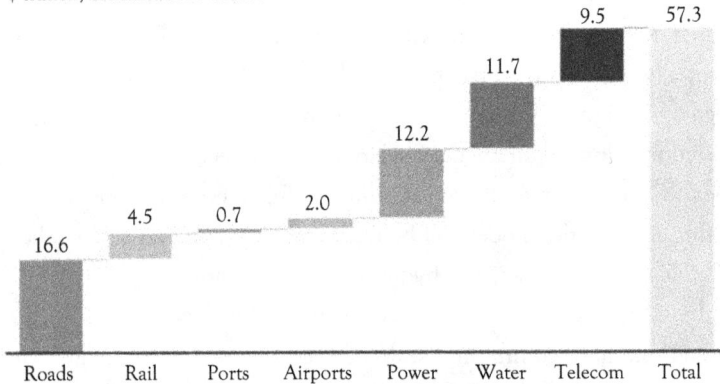

Roads	Rail	Ports	Airports	Power	Water	Telecom	Total
16.6	4.5	0.7	2.0	12.2	11.7	9.5	57.3

Figure 3.2 Investment required to meet global infrastructure demand by infrastructure segments through 2030.

Source: Exhibit from "Infrastructure productivity: How to save $1 trillion a year," January 2013, McKinsey Global Institute, www.mckinsey.com. Copyright (c) 2018 McKinsey & Company. All rights reserved. Reprinted by permission.

In the U.S., the 2016–2025 cumulative investment gap for electricity infrastructure is estimated to be $177 Billion, a figure that includes generation, and transmission and distribution (T&D).

The American Society of Civil Engineers periodically grades the U.S. on the state of its infrastructure. In 2017, the U.S. received cumulative infrastructure and energy grades of D+.[2] In 2017, there were 3,571 power outages lasting an average of 49 minutes. Clearly, the majority of America's electrical infrastructure is at or beyond its expected life.

Widespread national electrification occurred on the heels of the westward expansion of the 1800s. By 1930, about 70 percent of households

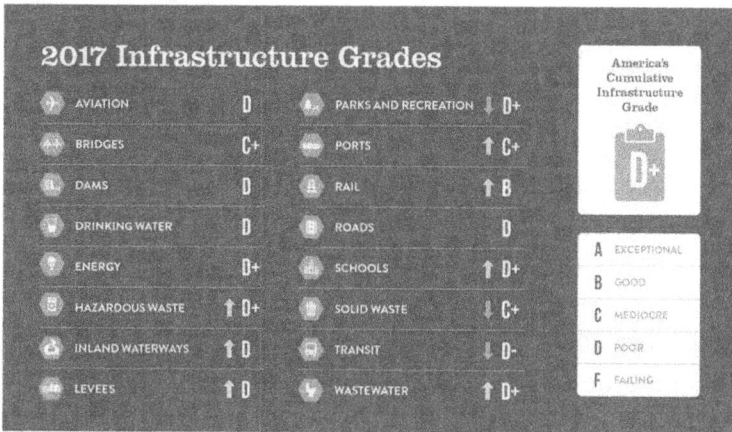

Figure 3.3 2017 Score card for US Infrastructure, as awarded by infrastructurereportcard.org.

were electrified, and electricity quickly became a public commodity. Most of the T&D lines that make up America's grid were constructed in the 1950s and 1960s and are now beyond their predicted 50-year life.

So, what is delaying an infrastructure upgrade? *The barrier to accessing capital is structural.* While investor-owned utilities (IOUs) make up only 6 percent of electricity providers in the U.S., they serve 68 percent of customers. Like other private entities, they are driven by short-term financial gain. This means that investment in T&D infrastructure must be economically justifiable. Electricity, however, is a public commodity, and rates are capped by regulators, making it difficult to justify investment. In addition, excess supply both from baseload and distributed renewable energy makes it challenging to raise rates.

As a rule of thumb:

- *Where demand > supply, pricing is high, investment is justified*
- *Where demand < supply, pricing is low, investment is constrained*

In the U.S., energy is generated and sold by a complex network of large and small public and privately-owned utilities, each subject to their own governance structures and energy pricing regulations.[3] The interactions between these entities are managed by *regional transmission organizations* and *independent system operators.*

- *Investor-Owned Utilities (IOUs)*: These companies hark back to the early days of Edison and Westinghouse, where energy was provided by companies held by shareholders and investors. The aim of a privately-owned company is to *optimize profits* and *maximize the returns* to its investors. However, IOUs are subject to regulation by local public entities that prevent them from raising energy rates as high as they would like (by issuing price caps via a public process).
- *Publicly-Owned Utilities (POUs)*: These utilities are owned and managed by local authorities or even by the customers themselves, if the POU is a cooperative. The aim of the POU is to provide the *best possible energy rates* for its customers, within the framework of managing overheads and debt. The organization's board (or depending on legal structure, the city council) agrees on energy rates within a public forum.

For both privately- and publicly-owned structures, maximizing returns to investors or customers takes precedence over costly long-term investments in infrastructure.

Developing Renewable Energy Projects

The first step for a developer is to make a case for capital. The National Renewable Energy Laboratory (NREL) describes the steps in this process as *Baseline, Economic, Policy, Technology, and Consensus (BEPTC)*.[4]

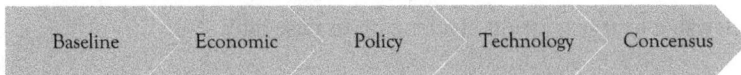

Baseline	Economic	Policy	Technology	Concensus

Figure 3.4 The National Renewable Energy Laboratory BEPTC framework.[5]

1. Baseline
The first step, the Baseline, requires the developer to outline a simple project motivation, for example to "reduce reliance on fossil fuels."

2. Economic
Next, the Economic rationale must be clearly established, and a positive return on investment demonstrated.

Since money has the potential to earn interest and the price of goods increases over time (inflation), a dollar you have today is worth more than a dollar in the future. _Net Present Value_ (NPV) is commonly used to assess the value of a project by returning the values of all future project earnings in today's dollars and subtracting the present value of all project costs. It is defined as the difference between the present value of an investment's future cash flows and the project's present and future costs.*

NPV = Present Value of Future Cash Flows – Present Value of Project Costs

If the project's worth today, or _NPV_, is positive, then the project makes financial sense. However, the economic analysis must include risk. The risk—reward relationship is directly proportional—the higher the risk, the greater the reward. We use the _Minimum Acceptable Rate of Return_ (MARR) to capture an investor's risk—reward profile—a high MARR indicates high risk and thus high expected returns.

If you were investing money in the stock market, what rate of return would you accept before putting your money into another investment? Corporate MARRs are very specific to the institution but generally vary from 10 to 20 percent. Investors have multiple options for their money so will direct their money to the most attractive investment.

Let's take an example. Say a new utility-scale solar PV system has a capacity of 1 MW and at $0.50/watt will cost $500,000 (1 MW * 1,000,000 watts/MW * $0.50). The array will produce 1,551 MWh (1 MW * 365 days * 5 peak sun hours * 0.85) and with an offtake agreement of $50/MWh, produce an annual value of $77,550 for 25 years (1,551 MWh * $50/MWh). Assuming a discount rate of 10 percent (reflecting a corporate MARR of 10 percent), the present value of the annual revenue over 25 years will be $703,924.45.

Therefore:

$$\textbf{NPV} = \$703,924.45 - \$500,000$$
$$= \$203,924.45$$

---

* See online resources for additional information on Time Value of Money calculations.

The NPV is positive and would be considered a good investment.

Another way to look at it is through a _Benefit-Cost Ratio_, which is simply the present value of the benefits divided by the present value of the costs. Many firms consider the investment only worthwhile if the benefits are at least two times greater than the costs. In this case:

$$\$703,924.45 \ / \ \$500,000$$
$$= 1.41$$

If the threshold were to double your investment, it would not be worthwhile.

Neglecting interest and inflation for a quick analysis, the simple payback period would be:

Payback (years) = Total Cost/Annual Revenue
$$= \$500,000/\$77,550$$
$$= \textbf{6.4 years}$$

The Return on Investment would be:

ROI = Annual Revenue/Total Cost
$$= \$77,550/\$500,000$$
$$= 0.16 * 100$$
$$= \textbf{16 percent ROI}$$

A final note—a comprehensive financial assessment must include a comparison of other investment options to determine the best investment of funds.

Large-scale renewable energy developers take advantage of private capital to realize their projects. _Debt Financing_ in the form of loans is most commonly used. _Equity Financing_ is more expensive, but investors are paid only after revenue is generated. Innovative delivery options exist to fund and manage public infrastructure through private capital. Known as _Public Private Partnerships_ (P3 or PPP), these agreements share risks, benefits, and expertise between government agencies and private entities.

Unlike conventional _Design Bid_ or _Design Bid Build_ contracts where all design, operations and maintenance risks remain with the public through taxes, P3 structures transfer risk to the private sector in exchange

Table 3.1 Types of public private partnership (P3) contracts and associated risks.

Types of public private partnership (P3) contracts		Risk transfer
Design Bid Build (DBB)	Separate contracts for design and construction	Public ——————— Private
Design Build (DB)	One contract for design and construction	Public ——————— Private
Design Build Operate Maintain (DBOM)	One contractor for design, construction, and O+M in exchange for fees from end users (common for highways and public transportation)	Public ——————— Private
Design Build Finance Operate (DBFO)	Same as DBOM except contractor finances O+M under a long-term lease (common for highways and public transportation)	Public ——————— Private
Build Own Operate (BOO), Build Own Operate Transfer (BOOT)	Contractor either owns or leases facility, provides financing and sells output (common in power sector)	Public ——————— Private

for more ownership and returns. These approaches are often piloted in emerging economies, such as India, China, Turkey and Lebanon, where governments leverage private capital to finance the massive infrastructure investments required for a burgeoning middle class.

An important element of the economic analysis is determining how the development project will generate income once the construction phase is complete. As previously discussed, energy project developers use power purchase agreements (PPAs) to sell their energy at a specified rate (cents/kWh) to *offtakers*, IOUs, or POUs under a Build Own Operate (BOO) or Build Own Operate Transfer (BOOT) contract. *Feed-in-Tariffs* (FiTs) of a set amount per kWh fed into the grid guarantee developers a high rate for renewable energy, and are a way for governments to stimulate renewable energy production without any upfront investment.

For instance, In 2009, the Government of Ontario, Canada implemented a FiT program as part of its Green Energy Plan. With the FiT, producers of energy from wind, solar, hydro and biomass/biogas were able to sign long-term contracts to supply power to the grid for prices up to 40 times the existing market value per kWh. (for residential PV under 10 kW the FiT was 80.2 cents per kWh for 20 years.) The program was "one of North America's first comprehensive guaranteed pricing structures for renewable electricity production"[6] and caused a boom in renewable energy production within the province. Some critics claim, however, that the high tariffs promised to green energy producers have contributed to Ontario's high energy prices for consumers. The program's final round of applications closed in 2016.[7]

Policy

Policy is particularly important for renewable energy projects. It takes into account existing *stakeholders* and *government incentives* or disincentives. Policy stakeholders span the spectrum from scientists involved in the design and fabrication of novel technology to government agencies that provide funding and regulatory structures. Research universities and laboratories house subject matter experts, such as physicists, chemists and engineers, who leverage their specific domains of expertise into practical technologies. In the U.S., the government can fund and regulate renewable energy at three levels: Federal, State and Local. The role of the Federal Government is to incentivize renewable energy deployment through incentives, and support innovation through funding R&D, through vehicles such as _Renewable Energy Credits (RECs)_, non-tangible energy commodities that can be traded or sold. The Federal Government can also disincentive fossil fuels through a _carbon tax_ or a _cap and trade system_.

State governments can similarly incentivize the development and adoption of green energy production through a _Renewable Portfolio Standard (RPS)_ and carve-outs. Solar carve-outs, for instance, are a component of an RPS, and require a percentage of a state's energy mix to come from solar by a certain date. Solar carve-outs include rules for solar energy interconnection and inter- and intra-state trading through _Independent System Operators_.

At the local level, _Authorities Having Jurisdiction (AHJs)_ set the rules for electrical, structural and mechanical design, and make the final permitting determinations.

At all levels, the utility is a central stakeholder. Utilities either secure PPAs from developers, own their own plants, or have off-take agreements, such as _Net Energy Metering_, with distributed generators. Other stakeholders include the community colleges that train technicians, manufacturers, distributors, testing and accreditation bodies such as Underwriters Laboratories (UL), the North American Board of Certified Practitioners (NABCEP), and the designers of software and tools used by engineers and technicians.

The electricity market itself is a stakeholder, since it affects renewable energy adoption. The electricity market includes both competitors and potential detractors, such as coal, oil and natural gas providers, complementary energy sources such as wind, and energy storage solutions like pumped hydro and batteries.

Finally, energy industry professionals are an important stakeholder. They are involved in the practical design, finance and installation of renewable energy systems. Financial entities, including renewable energy developers, lending institutions, and the stock market, can significantly hasten or slow the spread of renewable energy.

Scientists

- Research Universities
- Professors
- Physicists
- Material Scientists
- Electrical Engineers
- Chemists
- Chemical Engineers
- Mechanical Engineers

Government Agencies

- US Department of Energy
- NASA
- Federal Energy Regulatory Commission (FERC)
- State Energy Commissions
- Independent System Operators (ISO)
- Local Authorities Having Jurisdiction

Electricity Market

- Energy Prices (cents/kWh)
- Natural Gas Prices
- Natural Gas Peaker Facilities
- Pumped Hydro Facilities
- Utility-Scale Batteries
- Renewable Energy Industry

Industry Professionals

- Trainers
- Renewable Energy Installers/Electricians
- Architects
- Urban Designers
- Chemical Engineers
- Electrical Engineers
- Civil Engineers
- Mechanical Engineers
- Software Engineers

Financial

- Renewable Energy Developers
- Lending Institutions
- Stock Market

Industry

- Utilities
- Community Colleges
- Module Manufacturers
- Inverter Manufacturers
- Battery Manufacturers
- Balance of Systems
- Wholesale Distributors
- International Organization for Standardization (ISO)
- UL Certification
- NABCEP
- Design Software
- Design Tools

Users

- Humanity
- Residential, Commercial and Industrial Buildings
- Building Owners
- Utility PPAs
- Land Owners & Eminent Domain

Environment

- Human Welfare
- Environmental Impact
- Climate Change Mitigation

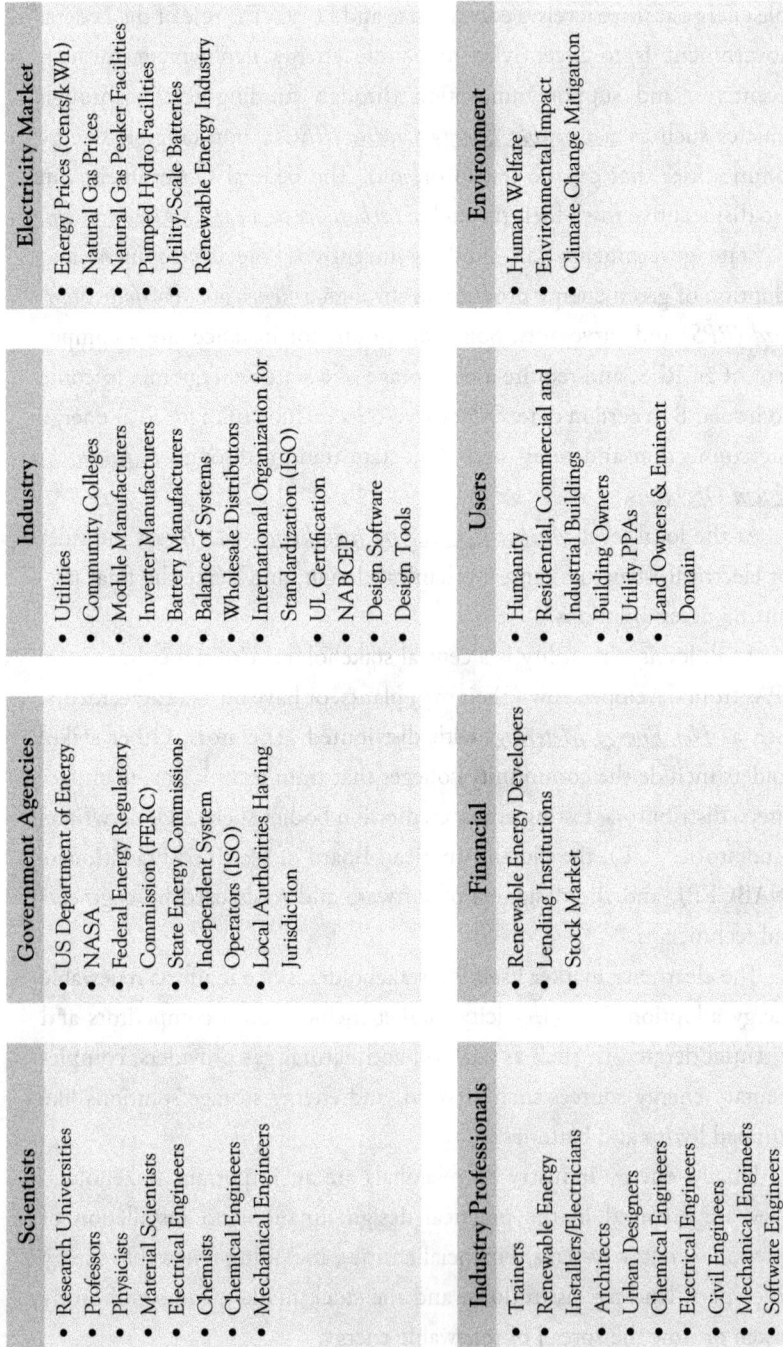

Figure 3.5 Key stakeholder groups and factors affecting the development and adoption of renewable energy.

3. **Technology**

The next stage of the BEPTC framework is to conduct a technology assessment. This involves a preliminary analysis of the resource and its economic potential, using the techniques outlined in Chapter 2.

4. **Consensus**

Before moving on to the construction phase, the developers must reach Consensus on the results of the Baseline, Economic, Policy and Technology analyses. Best practice is to engage with all project stakeholders listed above, including the _host community_. To create a Stakeholder Engagement strategy, the developer should map stakeholders on a Stakeholder Engagement Matrix according to their level of interest and influence, and engage with them accordingly throughout project development, construction, plant operation, and closeout.

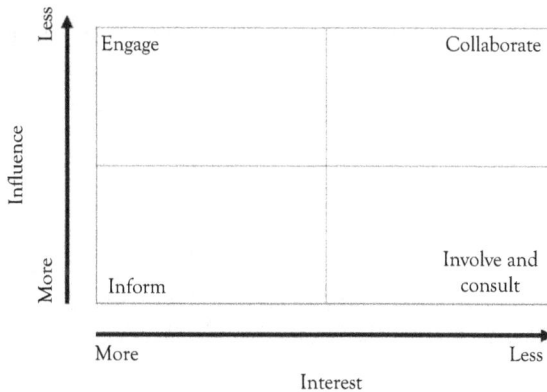

Figure 3.6 Stakeholder engagement matrix indicating the level of engagement required based on stakeholder influence and/or interest.

But why is consensus so important? On the one hand, for fairness, and on the other hand, for good business. All too often, a large investment in an energy infrastructure project will be developed to be Technically Feasible, Financially Viable and Environmentally Sustainable, with the relevant governmental, financial, technical and other stakeholders on board. But these projects fail to ensure that the local, or host communities, most impacted by the project, are also on board. Whether their landscapes and farmlands will be impacted by the view of and noise from a large wind farm,[8] or flooded by a dam for a new hydropower plant,[9] or even if the local community will experience short-term disruption from the construction of a large solar array, these local stakeholders must be consulted and their views taken into account during the project development phase; the project must be Socially Acceptable.

Taken together, this concept is known as Smart Business.[10] Without this level of consideration of host communities, interested and concerned protest and advocacy groups can cause serious delays to the construction of the project, costing thousands of dollars, and can even affect the political climate making the investment possible.

Constructing and Financing Renewable Energy Projects

Once consensus amongst all stakeholders is reached, the project can move on to the development phase, securing the _Site, Resource, Off-take, Permits, Technology, Team and Capital (SROPTTC)_.

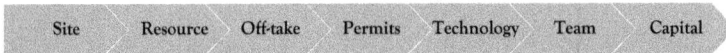

Site	Resource	Off-take	Permits	Technology	Team	Capital

Figure 3.7 SROPTTC Framework (National Renewable Energy Laboratory).[11]

Securing the _Site_ for the project involves obtaining property rights and fully understanding its physical properties. An _Investment-Grade_ assessment is conducted, building on the preliminary _Resource_ assessment done during the development phase. To do this, the resource needs to be fully understood, using detailed hourly data and computer modeling. The _Off-take_, or contracting method, for energy sales, must also be established.

Following _Environmental Assessments (EA)_, _permits_ must be secured. As mentioned, one type of permit that cannot be formally applied for and is often overlooked is known as the _Social License to Operate (SOL)_. As renewable energy projects can take up significant land and water resources and make an obvious impact on the landscape, it is important to secure and maintain a SOL through stakeholder engagement with affected parties before and during the construction phase, and through project closeout and operation.

Developers must make *Technological* selections to determine the project's primary components, and assemble a *Team* with complementary technical, financial, and project management skills. Then, *Capital* must be secured from investors, based on a proposal including all of the assessments completed.

Surmounting the Valley of Death

The challenge of securing funding for a new clean technology enterprise can seem insurmountable. The old adage "banks will always be the first in line to finance your second project" speaks to the challenge of attracting investment in innovative sectors. Developers need to not only secure capital for the start-up phase of the project (BEPTC and then SROPTT), but must also carefully manage the investment to avoid a cash flow crisis, known as *Death Valley*. This is the uncertain period between a venture's infancy and young adulthood in which initial R&D funding runs out, but revenue is not yet being generated.

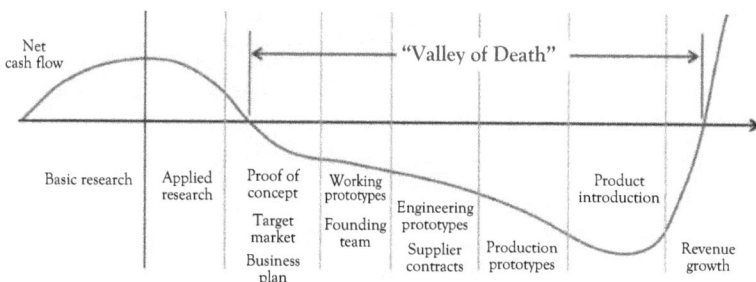

Figure 3.8 The "Valley of Death"—a period in which a new venture runs out of seed funding and before it generates revenue.

Source: https://www.go-gba.org/bridging-the-valley-of-death-and-crossing-death-valley/

New ventures follow a lifecycle called an *S Curve*. The shape comes from the three stages a product goes through toward successful commercialization: Innovation ("Startup"), Growth, ("Expansion") and Maturity ("Mature"). In the Innovation stage, efforts are focused on technological breakthroughs and market penetration is below 10 percent. During the Growth phase, market penetration and profit margins grow. Finally, in the Maturity stage, the product has reached above 90 percent penetration. During this stage, the market is saturated with the product, which lowers the cost and reduces profit margins. Typically, at this late stage companies have achieved significant _Economies of Scale_, the cost advantage from higher levels of production, which reduces manufacturing costs and mitigates decreased profit margins.

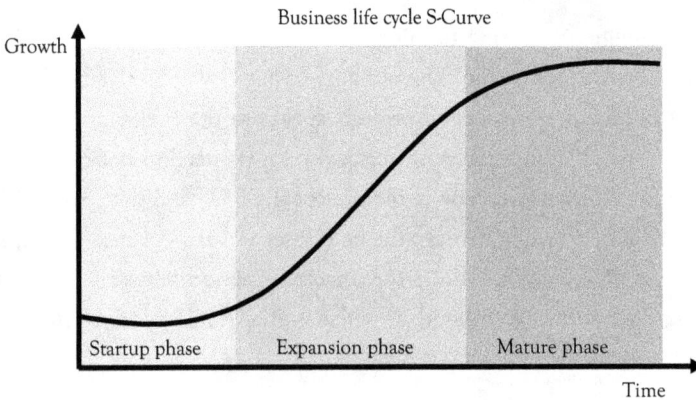

Figure 3.9 Business Life Cycle S-Curve.

Case Study 1: Curacao Stage One Utility-Scale Solar PV Assessment

The following case study illustrates a sample preliminary assessment for the development of a utility-scale solar energy project in Curaçao, an island off the coast of Venezuela in the former Kingdom of the Netherlands.

Brief

Curaçao is an autonomous constituent nation of the Kingdom of the Netherlands. A 444 km² island off the coast of Venezuela,[12] Curaçao's utility provider Aqualectra meets 70 percent of its 968,000 MWh (2008 estimate) needs through steam and gas turbines and diesel engines, and 30 percent through four wind turbine farms with a total rated power capacity of 60 MW.[13]

As of December 1, 2016, residential electricity rates ranged from $0.26 to $0.35/kWh[14,15] Given rising fuel costs, the island's abundant solar resource (5.5–6.2 peak sun hours, or 2,000–2,250 kWh/m² of annual solar radiation),[16] and decreasing solar PV costs ($1.50/watt for utility scale), Aqualectra should examine the business case for utility-scale solar PV.

This initial study examines potential sites that could contribute 30 percent of total demand (290,400 MWh) from solar PV and provide a MARR above 10 percent, reducing fossil fuel consumption to 40 percent. Given that wind and solar energy are complementary producers, with wind contributing more at night and solar more during the day, the introduction of solar PV would have a smoothing effect on power supply. Two sites were selected as each being capable of meeting this goal.

Assumptions

Production: To meet 30 percent of the island's needs, approximately 171 MW of installed PV capacity would need to be installed.[17]

Financial: The 171 MW system would cost approximately $256,500,000.[18] With an annual income of $81,312,000[19] the project would have a simple payback period of 3.2 years.[20] The net present value of the system with a life of 25 years and 10 percent discount rate would be $481,572,278 with a rate of return of 32 percent and an optimal benefit-cost ratio of 2.9.[21,22,23,24]

Methodology

Two sites were selected through factoring out the following factors: (1) low irradiance, (2) densely-populated areas, (3) uneven terrain, and (4) occupied land or land zoned for development or conservation (that is, natural parks). Two sites with the following optimal characteristics were thus selected: high irradiance, sparse population, even terrain, and unoccupied land.[25]

Site Selection

1. Irradiance

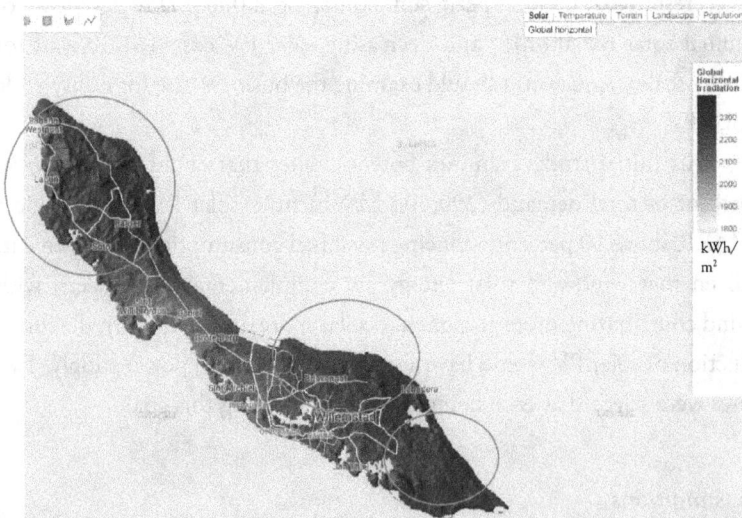

Figure 3.10 Optimal locations based on solar resource.

Source: SolarGIS.

To achieve the 5.5 daily peak sun hours, optimal sites include locations with >2,100 kWh/m²/year, as shown in the circles.

2. Population Density

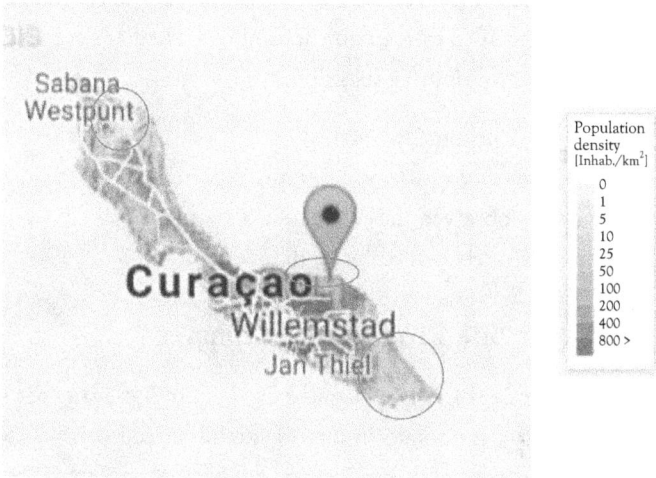

Figure 3.11 Optimal locations based on solar resource and low population density.

Source: Data from SolarGIS.

Examining population density narrowed site selection to three potential areas where there are less than five inhabitants/km², as shown.

3. Terrain

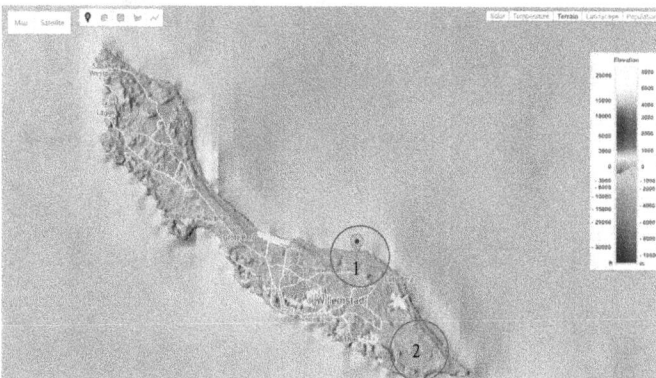

Figure 3.12 Optimal locations based on solar resource, population density, and level terrain.

Source: Data from SolarGIS.

The highest point in Curacao is Mt. Christoffel at only 1,227 feet above sea level. Areas with the most even terrain were visibly selected on the map above, identified by the two circles above. Further site inspection is necessary to confirm optimal selection.

4. **Land Status (Zoning/Ownership)**
   - Site 1's ownership and zoning status is currently unknown. The author observed the subject lot is vacant.
   - Site 2 is privately owned by an individual.

Site Production Estimates

Based on a system size of 171 MW and a capacity of 350 watts per module (high efficiency), the total number of modules needed is 488,572.[26] Given that the average module is 2 m² plus 0.5 m² for spacing, the total area needed is 1.22 km².[27]

Site 1—Northeast (Labadera/Santa Catharina)

Total area is 1.22 km², which can contain 488,571.43 modules and provide 171 MW. This site backs up to the Santa Catharina neighborhood. Consultation is likely necessary.

Figure 3.13 Site 1.

Source: Courtesy of Google Maps.

Site 2—East End

Total area is 1.22 km², which can contain 488,571.43 modules and provide 171 MW. This site is privately owned and undeveloped.

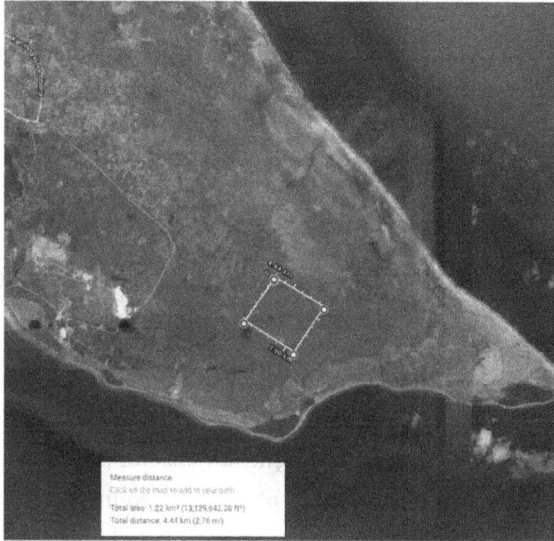

Figure 3.14 Site 2.

Source: Courtesy of Google Maps.

Next Steps

- Investigation of property ownership for selected areas.
- Physical inspection of sites to confirm optimal selection, including shading. Verify through NREL's System Advisor Model (SAM).
- Comprehensive estimate for solar PV system cost, including grid upgrades required.
- Consideration of upgrades to grid needed to accommodate solar PV system: battery storage (for when production exceeds demand), transmission infrastructure, voltage regulation, and so on.
- Comprehensive financial model to incorporate discount rates. Verify through NREL's SAM.
- Consideration of PPA and BOOT (build, own, operate, and transfer) mechanisms.

Case Study 2: Public Private Partnerships Enabling Hydropower Development in Lebanon

Elie Kallab, Fellow, UN Sustainable Development Solutions Network Youth Initiative

In light of Lebanon's 2020 goal of 12 percent renewable energy and recent legislation on public private partnerships (PPP), this case study examines the potential for further hydropower development in Lebanon through a PPP structure.

The Potential for PPP to Facilitate Hydropower Development in Lebanon

The rehabilitation and development of the hydropower sector in Lebanon requires extensive investment. In 2017, the Lebanese Parliament adopted PPP legislation, known as Law 48. The law ensures private sector establishments will be granted ownership of the land required for hydropower plants.[28,29] Prior to Law 48, the private sector was forbidden from owning hydropower plants, aside from small off-grid installations.

History of Hydro Power in Lebanon

Prior to the 1960s, Lebanon produced more than 60 percent of its energy from hydropower. Due to rising demand and increased generation from combined cycle gas-fired power plants, the hydropower capacity in Lebanon today is approximately 282 MW, only 8.7 percent of the country's total energy mix.[31] The state-run electric utility, Electricité du Liban (EDL), operates seven thermal plants fueled by gasoil, fuel oil, natural gas, and six hydropower plants.

Lebanon Energy Mix (as of 2014)

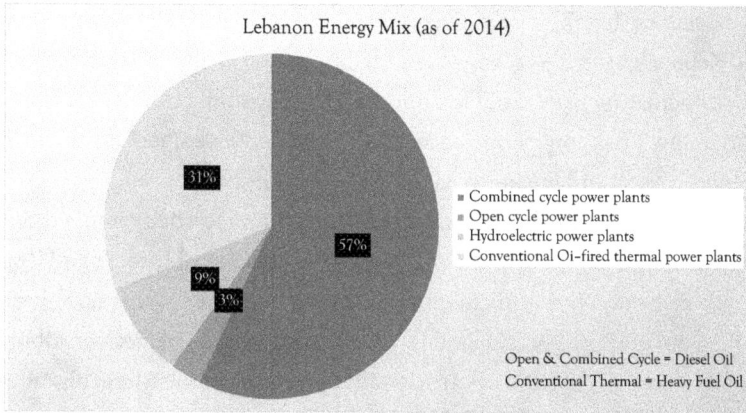

- Combined cycle power plants
- Open cycle power plants
- Hydroelectric power plants
- Conventional Oi–fired thermal power plants

Open & Combined Cycle = Diesel Oil
Conventional Thermal = Heavy Fuel Oil

Figure 3.15 Chart showing energy mix in Lebanon, based on figures from the Lebanese Republic Ministry of Energy and Water, 2014.[30]

Source: Data from Karim Osseiran, Ministry of Energy and Water Resources, Lebanese Republic.
https://www.slideshare.net/KarimOsseiran/geothermal-energy-potential-for-lebanon

Hydropower Potential in Lebanon

Lebanon is known for its seasonal changes. During the winter season, cyclonic depressions cause heavy rain and snowfall in the coastline and mountains of Lebanon. The summers are often without precipitation.

Average monthly rainfall in Beirut, Lebanon
from 1982 to 2012

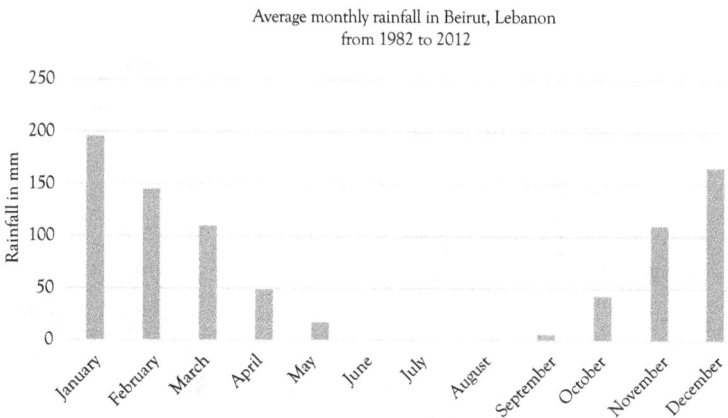

Figure 3.16 Monthly variability of rainfall in Lebanon.

Source: Climate-Data.org. https://en.climate-data.org/asia/lebanon/beirut/beirut-3572/

Lebanon has 17 major rivers, three of which are well-known: Nahr El Kebir, Nahr El Assi and Nahr El Hasbani. Lebanese Rivers experience fluctuating patterns of hydrologic flows due to the country's seasonal variability. Low flow periods occur from July to November and the high period runs from January to May.[32]

According to the World Bank, the demand for electricity in the country reached over 4,000 MW in 2015. Since the establishment of two combined cycle power plants in 1998, no new power plants have been added to meet rising demand. Current hydropower plants contribute approximately 282 MW of capacity. Of that capacity, the Markabi, Awali and Joun plant stations on the Litani Watani River Station contribute the most capacity, 199 MW.[33]

Conclusion

The private sector has the potential to rehabilitate existing publicly-owned hydropower plants and develop new river and non-river sources. According to the UNDP, private sector investment in hydropower would significantly increase power output at existing plants to 95.4 percent, hastening Lebanon's 2020 goal of 12 percent renewable energy.[34]

Chapter 3 Questions

1. What are the steps in renewable energy project development? Which step do you think is the most difficult to complete? How would you handle gaining community approval or a "social license to operate"? Debate in groups.

2. Which project delivery mechanism transfers the most risk to the private sector? Find an example of this mechanism being used for a renewable energy project and discuss its structure and implementation in groups. Do you think this mechanism is more common in certain countries? Why or why not?

3. A new utility-scale solar PV system has a capacity of 50 MW with a total installed cost of $0.50/watt. Assume 5 peak sun hours in your location, an offtake agreement of $50/MWh, a discount rate of 10 percent, and a system life of 25 years. What is the simple payback of your system?

4. For question 3, what is the net present value? What is the benefits-cost ratio? Is it a good investment?

5. Define the "S Curve." Research a renewable energy project development firm or technology firm. At which stage is the firm in the "S Curve"?

6. Brainstorm and research some strategies for overcoming the "Death Valley." Discuss in groups.

Chapter 3 Glossary

Authorities Having Jurisdiction (AHJ): an entity responsible for enforcing a code, or ensuring the standard of equipment, materials, installations and procedures.

BEPTC: The National Renewable Energy Laboratory framework for project development in the renewable energy sector, consisting of: Baseline, Economic, Policy, Technology and Consensus steps.

Cap and Trade System: also known as emissions trading, this system empowers emissions producers to manage their own response to national policy either through reducing their emissions and selling the remaining capacity to other producers, or maintaining emissions at the same rate and buying capacity from others.

Death Valley: an uncertain period in which a start-up runs out of initial R&D funding and revenue is not yet being generated from sales.

Debt Financing: Borrowing money from a bank or another company to finance a project in the form of a loan.

Environmental Assessments (EA): also known as Environmental Impact Assessments (EIAs), it is a thorough assessment of the environmental impact, both positive and negative, of a proposed project, as required by a local or national jurisdiction. EAs should include a level of public participation and decision-making.

Equity Financing: Raising money for a project by selling shares in it.

Feed-in-Tariffs: Guaranteed high offtake rates for renewable energy to spur investment.

Government Incentive: financial assistance (actual or in-kind) offered to private enterprise to promote a certain action. Includes tax breaks, grants, infrastructure sharing, and other resources.

Host Community: those who live close to and will be impacted by the energy generation plant, that is, a large PV installation, wind farm, or hydropower plant.

Independent System Operator: an entity responsible for managing a regional energy grid, as authorized by the Federal Energy Regulatory Commission (FERC).

Investment-Grade Audit / Assessment: a thorough examination of an energy resource or a facility's energy consumption to determine projects that will reap the greatest economic return.

Minimum Acceptable Rate of Return (MARR): An economic term defining an investor's risk tolerance. Generally, the greater the MARR, the more exposure to risk.

Net Energy Metering: an incentive similar to a feed-in-tariff, whereby small energy producers with grid-tie systems sell excess energy to the grid at the same retail electricity price at which they buy it.

Net Present Value (NPV): An economic term used to determine the profitability of an investment or project, describing the present value of a project's return on investment, minus the initial cost of the investment.

Offtaker: A party buying a product or service (in this case, energy).

Public Private Partnership (PPP): Long-term partnership between local authorities and private enterprise to deliver a project.

Renewable Energy Credit (REC): a tradable commodity that represents renewable energy production separate from the sale or use of the energy itself.

Renewable Portfolio Standard (RPS): a government regulation requiring a percentage of energy production come from renewable sources.

Site, Resource, Off-take, Permits, Technology, Team and Capital (SROPTTC): A framework for managing the physical construction of a renewable energy project, developed by the National Renewable Energy Laboratory.

Social License to Operate (SLO): The ongoing positive perception and approval of a project, its business practices and operations by its host community and employees. When a project is no longer perceived as positive, it may experience protests, boycotts, and applications for official permits to be removed. It can be very costly to restore a SLO once it has been lost.

Stakeholder: an individual or group with an interest, or "stake", in the matter at hand.

References

1. Dobbs, R., H. Pohl, D.Y. Lin, J. Mischke, N. Garemo, J. Hexter, S. Matzinger, R. Palter, and R. Nanavatty. 2013. *Infrastructure Productivity: How to save $1 Trillion a Year*. Publication. McKinsey Global Institute. https://mckinsey.com/~/media/McKinsey/Industries/Capital Projects and Infrastructure/Our Insights/Infrastructure productivity/MGI Infrastructure_Executive summary_ Jan 2013.ashx (accessed September 15, 2018).

2. Infrastructure Report Card 2017. "Publication. Infrastructure Report Card." https://infrastructurereportcard.org/wp-content/uploads/2017/01/Energy-Final.pdf (accessed September 15, 2018).

3. California Energy Commission. 2018. "Differences Between Publicly and Investor-Owned Utilities." http://energy.ca.gov/pou_reporting/background/difference_pou_iou.html (accessed September 15, 2018).

4. Springer, R. 2013. "A Framework for Project Development in the Renewable Energy Sector." Technical paper no. NREL/TP-7140-57963. National Renewable Energy Laboratory. *Golden, Colorado,* https://nrel.gov/docs/fy13osti/57963.pdf (accessed September 15, 2018).

5. Id.

6. "FIT Overview." *Ieso.ca,* http://ieso.ca/sector-participants/feed-in-tariff-program/overview

7. Hill, B. February 24, 2017. "Ontario Energy Minister Admits Mistake with Green Energy Program." *Global News,* https://globalnews.ca/news/3272095/ontario-energy-minister-admits-mistake-with-green-energy-program (accessed September 15, 2018).

8. Fleming, D. February 02, 2014. "Ireland's Rural Protests Over Wind Energy." *BBC News,* https://bbc.com/news/world-europe-25966198 (accessed December 03, 2018).

9. Bacchi, U. June 04, 2018. "Threatening Wilderness, Dams Fuel Protests in the Balkans." *Reuters,* https://reuters.com/article/us-bosnia-environment-

dams/threatening-wilderness-dams-fuel-protests-in-the-balkans-idUSKCN1J0007 (accessed December 03, 2018).

10. SMART Business Tools|AstonEco Management. 2018. "SMART Business Tools." https://astoneco.com/en/resources/smart-business-tools

11. Springer, R. 2013. "A Framework for Project Development in the Renewable Energy Sector." Technical paper no. NREL/TP-7140-57963. National Renewable Energy Laboratory. *Golden, Colorado: National Renewable Energy Laboratory.* https://nrel.gov/docs/fy13osti/57963.pdf (accessed September 15, 2018).

12. "The World Factbook: CURACAO." *Central Intelligence Agency,* https://cia.gov/library/publications/the-world-factbook/geos/cc.html (accessed December 10, 2016).

13. Aqualectra. 2016. "Can We Live with Wind Energy?" http://aqualectra.com/files/PDF/fly_energia_bientu_eng.pdf (accessed December 10, 2016).

14. Aqualectra. 2016. "Aqualectra Tariffs." http://aqualectra.com/files/Tarieven_2016/Dec_Valid_Tariffs_as_per_december_01_2016.pdf (accessed December 1, 2016).

15. All figures in USD.

16. Solar Gis Maps. 2016. "Solargis." *Satellite-derived Irradiance Database* http://solargis.info/imaps/#c=12.145325,-68.85915&z=11 (accessed December 10, 2016).

17. 171 MW * 365 days * 5.5 Peak Sun Hours * .85 (15 percent derating) = 291,790.13 MWh > 290,400 MWh.

18. Assuming a conservative $1.50/watt installed cost, $1.50/watt * 171,000,000 watts = $256,500,000.

19. 290,400,000 kWh production per year * $.28/kWh average charge to residential, commercial and industrial consumers = $81,312,000.

20. $256,500,000/$81,312,000 = 3.15 years.

21. NPV = PV of Annual Revenues − PV of Cost. PV of Annual Revenues of $81,312,000 over 25 years at 10 percent discount rate = $738,072,277.96. PV of Cost = $256,500,000. NPV = $738,072,278 - $256,500,000 = $481,572,278.

22. $81,312,000 income/$256,500,000 investment = .32 or 32 percent.

23. Analysis assumes vertical integration of investor-owned utility. PV plant will be owned and operated by Aqualectra. Analysis also assumes 100 percent utilization of power produced from PV system.

24. Benefit-cost ratio = PV of benefits/PV of costs = $738,072,278/$256,500,000 = 2.9.

25. A desert island, Curacao does not have to contend with heavily shaded areas. Therefore, this criterion was not taken into account. However, shading issues will be considered in the Stage Two Assessment.

26. 171,000,000 watts/350 watts = 488,571.43 modules.

27. 488,571.43 modules * 2.5m^2 = 1,221,428.57 m^2/1,000,000 = 1.22143 km^2.

28. Lebanese Parliament. September 9, 2017. "Official Journal." *Regulating Public Private Partnerships*. Beirut : Official Journal.

29. *Hydropower from Non-River Sources: The Potential in Lebanon*. Report. The Ministry of Energy and Water. Beirut, Lebanon: United Nations Development Program, 2013.

30. Osseiran, K. 2015. "Geothermal Energy Potential for Lebanon." *LinkedIn SlideShare*, June 01, 2015. https://slideshare.net/KarimOsseiran/geothermal-energy-potential-for-lebanon (accessed October 23, 2018).

31. *Hydropower from Non-River Sources: The Potential in Lebanon*. Report. The Ministry of Energy and Water. Beirut, Lebanon: United Nations Development Program, 2013.

32. Osseiran, K., S.M. Alaya, and V. Kabakian. 2013. *Hydropower in Lebanon; History and Prospects*. 4th ed. Report. CEDRO Exchange. Beirut, Lebanon: United Nations Development Program.

33. *Hydropower from Non-River Sources: The Potential in Lebanon*. Report. The Ministry of Energy and Water. Beirut, Lebanon: United Nations Development Program, 2013.

34. Lebanon targets 12% renewables in energy mix by 2020, https://aa.com.tr/en/energy/renewable/lebanon-targets-12-renewables-in-energy-mix-by-2020/8235

CHAPTER 4

Model 2: Distributed Renewable Energy Resources

In the previous chapter, we explored the development of grid-scale renewable energy projects. These large-scale projects, however, are no longer the only option. Remember Edison's original concept of decentralized generators? We may be coming around to his original plan in the second model of renewable energy development: On-site Power Generation.

Thanks to an increased interest in renewable energy production, and energy policies like the _Public Utility Regulatory Policy Act_ (PURPA), energy systems at the site of consumption are rivaling the traditional monopoly of utilities.

PURPA passed in 1978 in the U.S. to reduce U.S. dependence on foreign oil and to promote domestic energy production. PURPA required utilities to buy energy from _Non-Utility Generators_ (NUGs), disrupting their natural monopoly, and promoting alternative, renewable sources. In this framework, _Distributed Energy Resources_ (DERs), such as the grid-tie and grid-tie battery backup solar systems described in Chapter 2, emerged and are now reshaping the U.S. energy landscape.

In addition, the rapidly declining cost of solar energy has led to a surge in rooftop solar systems. These buildings remain connected to the grid, but generate electricity on-site to reduce their demand. The cost of solar energy systems have declined dramatically since the early 2010s, as shown in Figure 4.1, finally reaching _grid parity_, or cost equivalence, with conventional fuels.

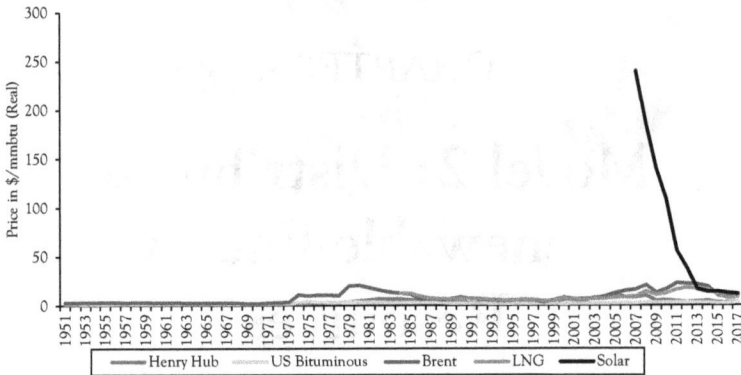

Figure 4.1 Price of energy production by energy type from 1949–
2012, showing the rapid reduction in cost of solar energy production
since the early 2010s.[1]

Source: Michael Parker and Flora Change, Bernstein; Data from EIA, CIA, and the World Bank

Basic research and improvements in the manufacturing process have
greatly reduced costs, from $76/watt in 1976 to $0.36/watt crystalline
silicon in 2018. Richard Swanson, founder of solar panel manufacturer
SunPower Corporation, noticed that PV module prices drop 20 percent
for every doubling of shipped volume. The trend is now called *Swanson's
Law*[2] and is shown in Figure 4.2.

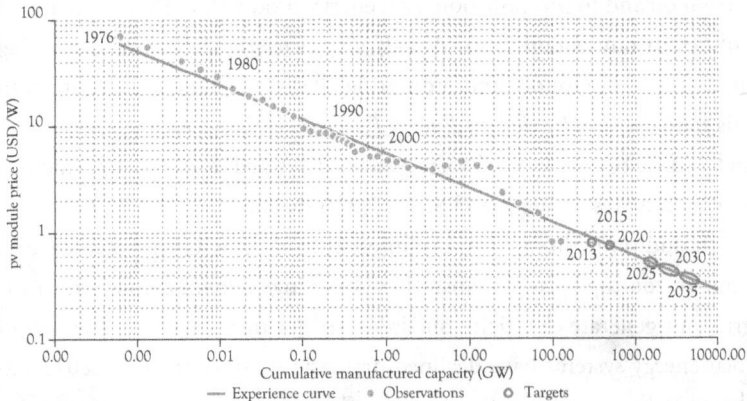

Figure 4.2 Swanson's law.

Source: IEA. https://www.iea.org/publications/freepublications/publication/TechnologyRoadmap
SolarPhotovoltaicEnergy_2014edition.pdf

Residential / On-Site Renewable Energy System Project Development

Interconnecting a grid-tie renewable energy system with the grid can be a complex process. In the U.S., permits are granted by local _Authorities Having Jurisdiction_ (AHJs), each with their own requirements. With over 18,000 AHJs in the U.S., this lack of standardization significantly increases the _soft costs_, or non-hardware costs, of installing a system.

For most small-scale solar PV systems (<10–15 kW), there is a simplified permitting process. Thanks to the work of Bill Brooks and the U.S. Department of Energy, many developers use the "Expedited Permit Process for PV Systems" or Solar ABCs in developing their permit application package.[3]

Following installation, the developer or installer submits a site plan, electrical diagram, and specification sheets to the AHJ. The AHJ will review and, sometimes, perform an inspection to ensure the array is compliant with all structural and electrical rules. Next, an _interconnection application_ is submitted to the utility along with the stamped permit. The utility checks that electrical protections (overcurrent protection devices-OCPDs, AKA circuit breakers) are in place to prevent energy export in the event of a grid outage, and to disconnect the system during a fault or short circuit. Once approved, the utility installs a bidirectional meter to determine net building consumption and the array may be "turned on," meaning the grid-tie inverter may now connect with the grid. In the case study at the end of this chapter, the author details the solar PV permitting process for a residential client in California.

Small-scale wind energy systems (</=100 kW) follow a similar review and permitting process, though are more complex due to the high variability of wind, as discussed in Chapter 2, and must consider proximity to airports. The Midwest Renewable Energy Association (MREA) has developed an excellent template "Small Wind Site Assessment Report," which details the standard requirements.*

---

* This template is available in the online resources for this book.

Financing Distributed Renewable Energy Resources

Numerous financing options have emerged in recent years for small-scale renewable energy systems.

Small Scale Financing Options

Similar to purchasing a car, home or business, owners can purchase a solar or wind energy system through a *zero-down lease* or power purchase agreement (PPA). In the case of a lease, one pays a leasing company a fixed monthly fee based on the estimated production of the system. In the case of a PPA, the beneficiary hosts power generating equipment and pays a fixed price per kWh to the provider for the energy produced by the system. The business model, known as *Solar as a Service (SaaS)*, was first introduced in 2007 by Sunrun. While this service offsets the steep initial cost, it essentially replaces the utility with a third-party service provider and costs more long term than if the user owned the system.

Commercial and Industrial Financing Options

Commercial and industrial energy projects involve more complex financing than residential installations. One technique used to attract debt or equity financing is *warehousing*, packaging multiple renewable energy projects together into one investment opportunity, which reduces risk to investors through diversification.[4] To enter into a warehouse, an energy project must already have a long-term PPA in place, assuring the investor that there is a market for the energy that will be produced. Warehousing is a way of developing funding during the high-risk development and construction phase of an energy project. Once the asset is fully constructed and generating power, it is often transferred to a *Yieldco*.[5]

Yieldcos are funds of aggregated renewable energy projects with predictable, long-term PPAs. They allow investors to earn tax-free dividends from consistent cash flows, as a result of guaranteed income from the projects' PPAs, and renewable energy subsidies. Yieldco expansion is made possible by regular absorption of new projects, often developed within a warehousing agreement, as part of a pipeline or drop-down schedule. In the U.S., yields are at about 7 percent, and, in the UK, 6 percent.[6]

As more homeowners seek to fully own their systems, _asset-backed securitization_ is becoming more popular. Securitization is the process of valuing a portfolio of renewable energy assets based on their PPA cash flows and making them tradeable instruments with their own monetary value, or "securities." You may remember the Great Recession of 2008, when sub-prime mortgages were securitized, and the "bubble burst" when home prices plummeted. Renewable energy projects are far less speculative as cash flows from kWh sales are assured.[7]

Another innovative finance method is the _Energy Savings Performance Contract (ESPC)_ that allows organizations to make improvements to their energy usage/generation systems with no up-front costs, and to pay for their system over time through their energy savings. This funding mechanism is commonly employed in U.S. Government construction and renovation projects and begins with energy conservation measures, followed by on-site renewable energy systems to achieve _net zero_—a state in which a building's energy consumption is 100 percent offset by all efficiency measures and renewable onsite production. The split varies by facility but is usually 75 percent demand reductions from energy efficiency and 25 percent generation from on-site renewable energy.

Combined, these financing mechanisms are helping to unlock the capital that is dramatically lowering the _levelized cost of energy (LCOE)_, a method for comparing the relative cost of energy produced by different sources. LCOE shows the cost of every unit of energy in $/kWh. This is an important measure for understanding _grid parity_, renewable energy generating power at a price equivalent to or less than the price of purchasing power from the grid, assuming the grid is primarily from fossil fuels.

LCOE = Life Cycle Cost / Lifetime Energy Production[8,9]

Life Cycle Cost (LCC) = Project Cost – Investment Tax Credit (ITC)* + O&M + Loan Payments – Present Value of Performance Incentives[†]

---

* The US ITC for residential PV will continue at 30 percent until 2020 when it will decline to 26 percent.

† Performance-Based Incentives vary by country, province and state. Generally they include Renewable Energy Credits and carbon credits. System owners can sell these products to firms seeking to support renewable energy or become carbon neutral.

Let's take an example of a house that consumes 10,000 kWh/year and has 5 peak sun hours, requiring a PV array of 6.5 kW. The system will produce 10,083 kWh/year. Over a 25-year life it will produce 252 MWh (See Chapter 2 for more detail on how to do these calculations). Assume the inverter will be replaced once in the system's lifetime, which adds $0.40/watt to O&M. Assume the system is owned so there will be no loan payments, and that the owner receives $0.10/kWh for performance incentives. Also, assume a 10 percent discount rate.

Components of Lifecycle Cost
Project Cost = $19,500 ($3/watt * 6,500 watts).
ITC = $5,850 (30% of $19,500)
O&M = $2,600 ($0.40/watt * 6,500 watts)
Loan Payments = $0
Present Value of Performance Incentives = $9,152.38 (10,083 kWh per year * $0.10/kWh = $1,008.30/year over 25 years at 10 percent discount rate)

Without the performance incentives
Life Cycle Cost = $16,250

Levelized Cost of Energy = $16,250 / 252,000 kWh
= $0.06/kWh

With the performance incentives
Life Cycle Cost =$7,097.62
Levelized Cost of Energy = $7,097.62 / 252,000 kWh
= $0.03/kWh

Considering that the average cost of electricity in the U.S. is $0.12/kWh, this LCOE is well below grid parity!

As explored, greater access to capital is transforming the electrical grid from a centralized utility with distributed customers to a decentralized web of *prosumers*, former consumers who are now also contributing to the grid. In the next chapter, we will discuss the final and newest model of interconnection, characterized by prosumers aggregating into communities of shared local resources and networks called microgrids.

Case Study: Permit Process for Grid-Tie PV System in California

In 2016, the author designed a 6 kW grid-tie solar PV system for a residential client in Fairfield, CA, 50 miles east of San Francisco. From site assessment and design to permitting and interconnection, this case study illustrates the steps and complexities involved in the process of designing and interconnecting a residential grid-tie solar PV system.

Pre-permit Package

The first step was to perform a site assessment to determine the optimal location for a PV array. This involved identifying rooftop obstructions and running a shading simulation using Helioscope.* Along with Helioscope, Aurora Solar is often used by solar energy designers.

Next, the author developed a site plan, and demonstrated that the structural and electrical requirements met the AHJ's standards. Equipment

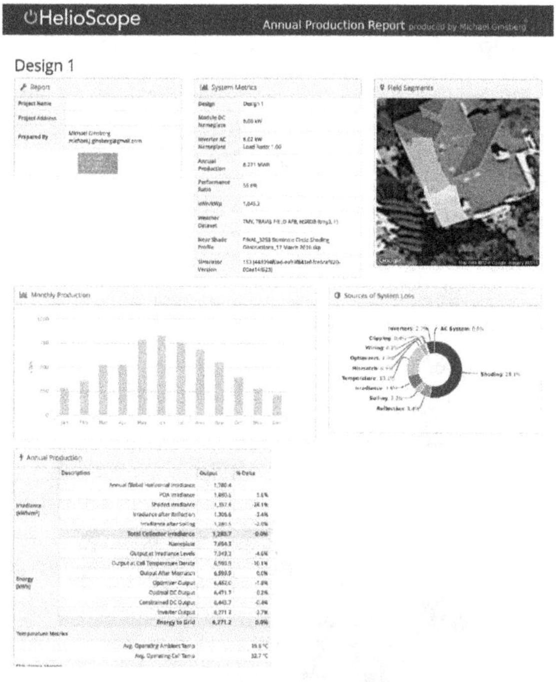

Figure 4.3 Draft design for a household PV system.

Source: Author and HelioScope

---

* See online resources for this book for shading simulation sample.

manufacturer specification sheets were provided in an appendix, with relevant information circled. The following are sections from the actual permit application.

Permit Package Section 1: Project Information

System Description: The array consists of a 6 kW DC roof-mounted PV power system operating in parallel with the utility grid. There are (24) 250-watt modules that run in series in two power optimizer strings to (1) 6 kW string inverter. The array is mounted to a roof comprised of concrete tile using the engineered racking solution from Everest with Flat Tile Roof Hooks-90 degrees from Solar Roof Hook.

System Specifications

- **String Inverter**—SolarEdge SE6000A-US (1)
- **Modules**—Boviet 250 Polycrystalline silver BVM6610P_09252015 (24)
- **Power Optimizers (Module Add on)**—SolarEdge Power Optimizer P300 (24)
- **Railing**
  - Everest CrossRail 48-S, 166" Mill (14pc)
  - Mounts(46 #17542) with screws
  - Mid clamps: 26pc
  - End clamps: 18pc
  - Rail splice: 8pc (with bolts)
  - MC4 connectors: 10 pack male/female
- **Attachment System**
  - Flat Tile Roof Hooks 90 Degree 38 mm and kit (20 hooks)

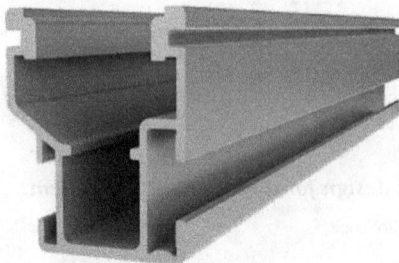

Figure 4.4 Railing: Everest Crossrail 48-S.

Permit Package Section 2: Structural

Figure 4.5 below shows the nearest climatological data for the region, including the daily average wind speed and gust, and maximum peak gust. At a minimum, the array must be designed to withstand maximum wind speeds greater than the maximum peak gust. Often, AHJs specify much higher gusts, as does the City of Fairfield.

STATION: NAPA COUNTY AIRPORT (KAPC), CA

CLIMATOLOGICAL SUMMARY. Period of Record: May 1998 to Dec 2008

Summaries based on unedited daily ASOS data. Errors may be present.

WIND (MPH)	Jan	Feb	Mar	Apr	May	Jun	Jul	Aug	Sep	Oct	Nov	Dec	Year
Daily Avg Wind Speed	6.8	6.5	7.1	8.5	9.1	9.9	9.9	9.1	7.4	6.0	5.5	6.6	7.7
Daily Avg Max 2-Min	16.9	16.9	18.2	20.5	19.9	20.2	19.2	18.5	17.0	15.9	15.2	16.9	17.9
Daily Avg Peak Gust	20.1	20.0	21.4	24.4	23.5	23.4	22.3	21.6	19.8	18.7	18.2	20.4	21.2
Maximum Daily Avg	18.2	19.2	18.0	17.3	20.2	17.9	15.9	15.5	14.3	20.4	16.4	18.0	20.4
Maximum 2-Minute Avg	39	41	41	38	32	38	29	32	31	34	41	37	41
Date of Max 2min-Day	04	28	01	08	02	05	26	12	17	21	24	16	
-Year	2008	2002	2002	2005	2001	2007	2000	2008	2004	2000	2001	2002	
Maximum Peak Gust	52	49	48	46	39	44	33	61	38	43	59	51	61
Date of Max Gust-Day	04	28	01	08	02	05	20	12	22	21	08	16	
-Year	2008	2002	2002	2005	2001	2007	2000	2008	2006	2000	2008	2002	
Avg Number of Days:													
Peak Gust >=30	3.0	3.9	3.8	5.9	4.8	2.8	2.3	1.4	1.0	1.6	2.1	3.8	36.4
Peak Gust >=40	0.3	0.6	0.1	0.7	0.0	0.1	0.0	0.1	0.0	0.2	0.3	0.5	2.8
Peak Gust >=50	0.1	0.0	0.0	0.0	0.0	0.0	0.0	0.1	0.0	0.0	0.2	0.1	0.5
Max 2-Minute >=30	1.1	0.9	1.0	1.5	0.8	0.3	0.0	0.2	0.2	0.3	0.6	0.0	6.8
Max 2-Minute >=40	0.0	0.1	0.1	0.0	0.0	0.0	0.0	0.0	0.0	0.0	0.1	0.0	0.3

Observations of WEATHER may me innacurate due to early ASOS inconsistancies. Average days with Thunderstorms may be low due to early mis-detection.

Heavy Fog = Visibility less than or equal to 1/4 mile.
Fog = Visibility greater than 1/4 mile or less than 7 miles.
Peak Gust = Maximum 5-second average.
Snowfall data not observed at ASOS stations.

Copyright ©2009 Western Regional Climate Center · Desert Research Institute · Reno, Nevada.

Figure 4.5 Napa County Airport, CA Wind Speed Data (16 miles SW of Fairfield, CA 94534).[10]

Daily Mean Speed: 7.7 MPH; Maximum Peak Gust: 61 MPH (registered in August 2008)

Source: Courtesy of Western Regional Climate Center, Desert Research Institute.

Figure 4.6 shows the maximum span length across a roof pitched 0 to 7 degrees based on ultimate (maximum) wind speeds expected in the region and expected snow load in pounds per square feet (psf). Exposure C means open terrain with scattered obstructions having heights less than 30 feet. Using the information above, we know the ultimate wind speed is 61 MPH, which is less than the lowest category of 110 MPH. Also, the city of Fairfield states the wind design criteria is 110 MPH and Exposure C.[11]

Table 1.5: Maximum Span Length (in.) - Wind Exposure C Condition

Exposure	Ultimate Wind Speed, V (mph)	Rail Type	Roof Wind Pressure Zone 1 Roof Snow Load (psf)						Roof Wind Pressure Zone 2 Roof Snow Load (psf)						Roof Wind Pressure Zone 3 Roof Snow Load (psf)					
			0	10	20	30	40	50	0	10	20	30	40	50	0	10	20	30	40	50
C	110	X80	128	118	108	99	87	78	115	115	108	99	87	78	93	93	93	93	87	78
		X48	94	88	81	72	63	56	79	79	79	72	63	56	64	64	64	64	63	56
		48-S	90	85	73	63	55	50	71	71	71	63	55	50	57	57	57	57	55	50
	115	X80	128	118	108	99	87	78	110	110	108	99	87	78	89	89	89	89	87	78
		X48	92	88	81	72	63	56	75	75	75	72	63	56	61	61	61	61	61	56
		48-S	87	85	73	63	55	50	67	67	67	63	55	50	55	55	55	55	55	50
	120	X80	128	118	108	99	87	78	105	105	105	99	87	78	85	85	85	85	85	78
		X48	89	88	81	72	63	56	72	72	72	72	63	56	58	58	58	58	58	56
		48-S	85	85	73	63	55	50	65	65	65	63	55	50	52	52	52	52	52	50
	130	X80	123	117	107	99	87	78	97	97	97	97	87	78	79	79	79	79	79	78
		X48	84	84	80	72	63	56	66	66	66	66	63	56	54	54	54	54	54	54
		48-S	78	78	73	63	55	50	59	59	59	59	55	50	48	48	48	48	48	48
	140	X80	117	115	106	99	87	78	90	90	90	90	87	78	73	73	73	73	73	73
		X48	79	79	79	71	63	56	61	61	61	61	61	56	50	50	50	50	50	50
		48-S	72	72	71	63	55	50	55	55	55	55	55	50	45	45	45	45	45	45
	150	X80	109	109	104	97	87	78	84	84	84	84	84	78	68	68	68	68	68	68
		X48	75	75	75	69	63	56	57	57	57	57	57	56	46	46	46	46	46	46
		48-S	67	67	67	61	55	50	51	51	51	51	51	50	42	42	42	42	42	42
	160	X80	102	102	102	96	87	78	78	78	78	78	78	78	64	64	64	64	64	64
		X48	70	70	70	68	62	56	54	54	54	54	54	56	43	43	43	43	43	43
		48-S	63	63	63	60	55	50	48	48	48	48	48	48	39	39	39	39	39	39
	170	X80	96	96	96	94	86	78	74	74	74	74	74	74	60	60	60	60	60	60
		X48	66	66	66	66	61	56	50	50	50	50	50	50	41	41	41	41	41	41
		48-S	59	59	59	59	54	50	45	45	45	45	45	45	37	37	37	37	37	37
	180	X80	91	91	91	91	84	78	70	70	70	70	70	70	57	57	57	57	57	57
		X48	62	62	62	62	60	56	47	47	47	47	47	47	39	39	39	39	39	39
		48-S	55	55	55	55	53	49	43	43	43	43	43	43	35	35	35	35	35	35
	200	X80	81	81	81	81	81	76	62	62	62	62	62	62	51	51	51	51	51	51
		X48	55	55	55	55	55	54	43	43	43	43	43	43	35	35	35	35	35	35
		48-S	50	50	50	50	50	48	38	38	38	38	38	38	31	31	31	31	31	31

ROOFS 0° TO 7°

Figure 4.6 Diagram showing the maximum span length across a roof pitched 0 to 7 degrees based on ultimate (maximum) wind speeds expected in the region and expected snow load in pounds per square feet (psf).

Source: Kelley, Shawn P. Moment Engineering + Design for Everest Solar Systems LLC

The rail type is 48-S and, according to the National Oceanic and Atmospheric Administration (NOAA), the region has a roof snow load in pounds per square feet (psf) of 0.[12]

Roof Wind Pressure Zone refers to the area of the roof subjected to the wind load. As shown in Figure 4.7, Zone 1 is interior, and since it is the largest area, accounting for about 80 percent of the roof surface, it has the lowest load. Zone 2 are end zones, the roof perimeter, and account for 15 percent of the surface, and thus have a higher load. Zone 3 are corners, account for 5 percent of the surface, and have the highest load.

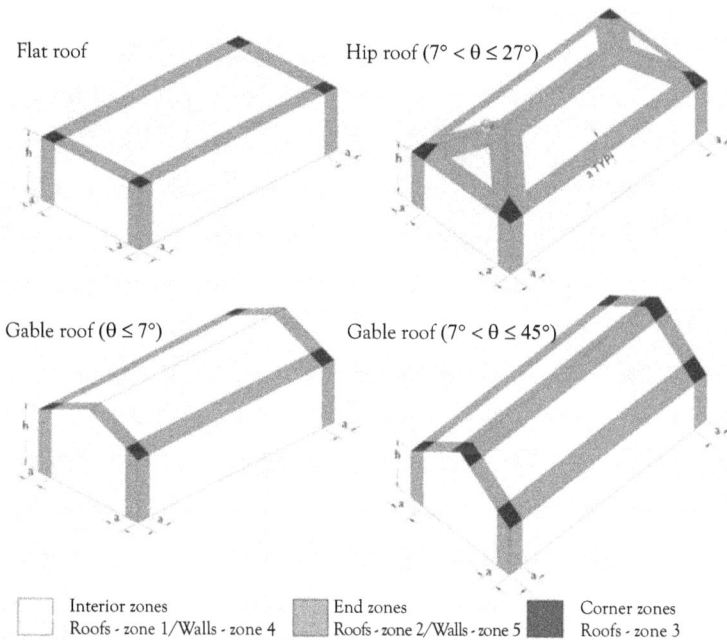

Flat roof   Hip roof ($7° < \theta \leq 27°$)

Gable roof ($\theta \leq 7°$)   Gable roof ($7° < \theta \leq 45°$)

Interior zones	End zones	Corner zones
Roofs - zone 1/Walls - zone 4	Roofs - zone 2/Walls - zone 5	Roofs - zone 3

Figure 4.7 Roof types.

The author's client has a Gable Roof of 0 to 7 degrees pitch and the site assessment revealed the array will be installed on the roof interior, *Zone 1.* As shown in Figure 4.6, there is an inversely proportional relationship between zone and maximum span length—as you increase the zone number from interior to corners, you decrease maximum span length. It should be noted the majority of PV systems are in Zone 1.

Therefore, consulting the maximum span length table (Figure 4.6), we can determine that the *maximum span length is 90 inches, or 7.5 feet.*

Attachment System: F-Tile Solar Roof Hook

The roof hooks shown in Figure 4.8 were used to attach the above railing to the client's engineered composite roof. Spacing between hooks was followed as specified by the manufacturer.

FLAT TILE ROOF HOOK
FOR SIDE MOUNT RAILS; NON-ADJUSTABLE

QuickB⬡LT

Part #	Box Quantity	Screw Size
17540	20 Hooks	N/A
17541	1 Hook	N/A
17542	20 Hooks; 40 Screws	#14 x 3"
17543	1 Hook; 2 Screws	#14 x 3"
17608	20 Hooks; 40 Screws	5/16" x 3"
17609	1 Hook; 2 Screws	5/16" x 3"

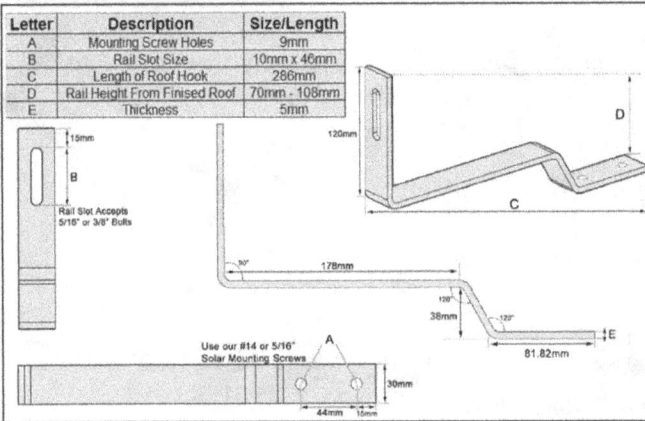

Letter	Description	Size/Length
A	Mounting Screw Holes	9mm
B	Rail Slot Size	10mm x 46mm
C	Length of Roof Hook	286mm
D	Rail Height From Finised Roof	70mm - 108mm
E	Thickness	5mm

Rail Slot Accepts
5/16" or 3/8" Bolts

Use our #14 or 5/16"
Solar Mounting Screws

5830 Las Positas Road, Livermore CA 94551 | 3948 Airway Drive, Rock Hill SC 29732
Phone: (844) 671-6045 | Fax: (800) 689-7975 | www.quickbolt.com
QuickBOLT is a division of Quickscrews International Corp.

Figure 4.8 Roof Hooks used to attach rail to engineered composite roof. *

---

* For specifications refer to: https://solarroofhook.com/sites/solarroofhook.com/files/reports/pdfFiles/17540spec_0.pdf

For installation guide refer to manual:https://solarroofhook.com/sites/solarroofhook.com/files/flat_tile_install_instructions_2-small.pdf

Or video: https://youtube.com/watch?time_continue=22&v=hSW7dFLrYls

Permit Package Section 3: Roof Plans (Showing 3' Setbacks and Roof Attachment Points)

Fairfield, CA required detailed roof plans with dimensions. Three-foot setbacks, space from the ridge and one and a half feet from hips or valleys if modules are on both sides, were required to allow walking space for firefighters and other safety personnel to access the system. These setback rules are particular to CA. In 2018, the three-foot requirement was modified to one and a half feet to allow for more modules on the roof. This is an ongoing debate between the solar energy and fire protection communities.[13]

The author created a 3D roof plan using Google Maps, illustrating the placement of modules, rafters, hooks, and dimensions, shown in Figure 4.9.

- 3D Roof Plan (not to scale)
- Detail 1 (scaled)
- Detail 2 (scaled)
- Detail 3 (scaled)

Figure 4.9 3D roof plan illustrating the placement of PV modules, rafters and hooks. Details 1, 2 and 3 show the scaled placements of PV modules, rafters, hooks and attachments on each segment of the roof.

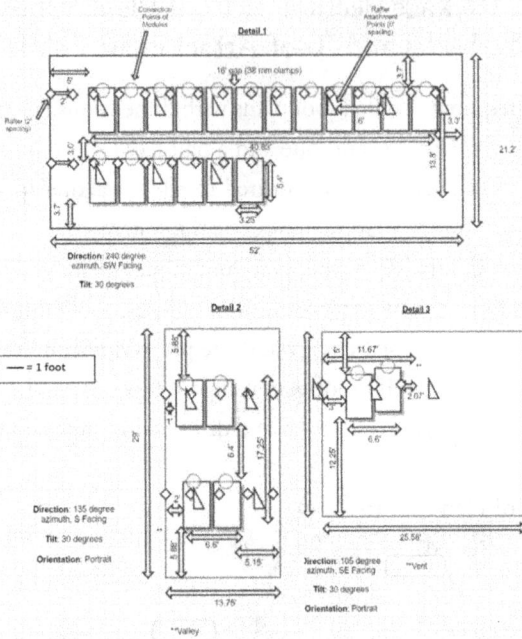

Figure 4.9 (Continued)

Permit Package Section 4: Electrical

Figure 4.10 shows the one line diagram and electrical details for the 24 module array using the SolarABCs template described above. The author sized the system using the string system maximum voltage sizing method detailed in Chapter 2.* Also, the author included electrical specifications of the modules and balance of systems (inverters and OCPDs).[14]

Once the City of Fairfield Building and Fire Safety Division reviewed and stamped the package, an inspector visited the site and completed the construction and building inspection permit. Next, the author completed and submitted interconnection application forms to the utility, Pacific Gas & Electric (PG&E). These are shown in Figures 4.11 and 4.12. This form applies to systems of 30 kW or less interconnecting with the grid.

---

* Although the steps involved in determining all of the electrical specifications of a PV array are outside the scope of this book, the author has included several useful references on the online site for this book.

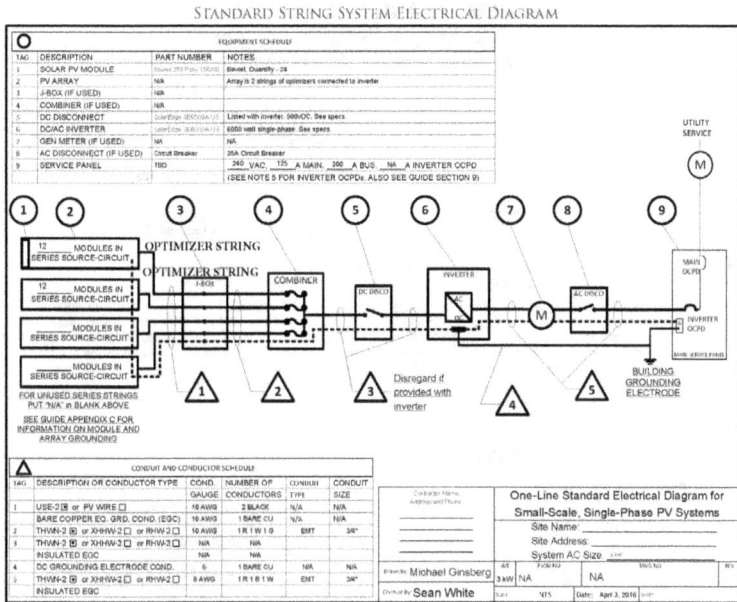

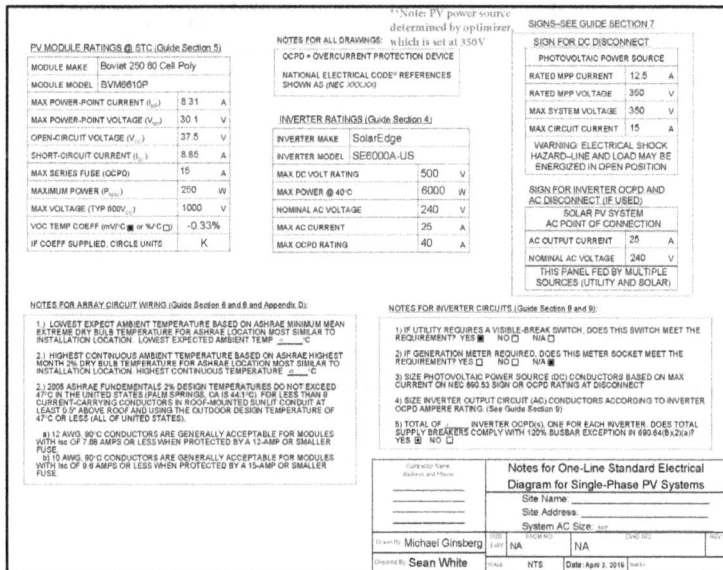

Figure 4.10 One line diagram and electrical details for a 24 module solar array.

Source: Author, Expedited Permitting Process, Solar ABCs http://www.solarabcs.org/about/publications/reports/expedited-permit/

AGREEMENT AND CUSTOMER AUTHORIZATION
Net Energy Metering Interconnection
For Solar And/Or Wind Electric Generating
Facilities Of 30 Kilowatts Or Less

Pacific Gas and Electric Company

Part II – NEM Generator System Size

A. Interconnection Study and Requirements

This Agreement covers the installed Generating Facility nameplate listed in the accompanying Application Form 79-1151B.

The interconnection study will use the nameplate to determine if Interconnection Facilities or Distribution or Network Upgrades are required and the responsible party for the associated costs. If upgrades are required, this will increase the time it will take for PG&E to approve your interconnection.

In order for PG&E to approve your system, you will need to provide (1) this signed Agreement, (2) Application Form 79-1151B, and (3) a copy of the final signed jurisdiction approval (building permit) for your project.

NEM systems should be sized with an estimated annual production no larger than 110% of the Customer's total previous 12 months of usage (annual usage) and projected future increase. For customers on a Time-of-Use rate, sizing your system to offset 80%-85% of your average electricity usage could be an effective way to minimize your electricity bill. For customer who are not on a Time-of-Use rate, you might want to size your system larger (90-95% of your annual load), in order to minimize your electricity bill. Of course, individual circumstances may vary. Customers can obtain their usage data from www.pge.com/greenbutton. System sizing eligibility will be reviewed using the criteria below.

B. Generator System Sizing

Generator System Type: ☒ Solar   ☐ Wind   ☐ Both

Estimated Annual Production:

- Solar Systems > 5 kW (CEC-AC kW) or any system with wind, size is determined below. Please continue to fill out all of Section B.
- The Solar CEC-AC kW calculated from the Application cannot exceed 5% of the CEC-AC kW listed above

(1) Solar CEC-AC rating[A]	5.850 (kW) X 1,664[B] =	9,734 (kWh)
AND/OR (2) Wind Nameplate rating	(kW) X 2,190[C]	(kWh)
(3) Total Energy Production	(1) + (2)	9,734 (kWh)

Estimated Annual Energy Usage:

(4) Recent annual usage	15,590 (kWh) X 1.1 =	17,149 (kWh)
OR (If 12 months usage not available) (5) Building size	(sq ft) X 3.32[D] =	(kWh)
AND (6) I plan to increase my annual usage (kWh) by		0 (kWh)
(7) Total Energy Usage	(4 or 5) + (6) =	17,149 (kWh)

Net Generation:

(8) Production - Usage	(3) – (7) =	-7,415 (kWh)*

*Positive number indicates that the system is estimated to generate more than the estimated usage. Please refer to Part IV, Section J to read the provisions around Net Surplus Compensation (NSC).

[A] CEC-AC (kW) =California Energy Commission Alternating Current, refers to the inverter efficiency rating (Quantity of PV Modules x PTC Rating of PV Modules x CEC Inverter Efficiency Rating)/1000
[B] 8,760 hrs/yr x 0.19 solar capacity factor = 1,664
[C] 8,760 hrs/yr x 0.25 wind capacity factor = 2,190
[D] 2 watts/sq ft x 1/1,000 watts x 8,760 hrs/yr x 0.19 solar capacity factor = 3.32

Please complete this agreement in its entirety
Automated Document, Preliminary Statement, Part A.

Page 2 of 6
Form 79-1151A
Advice 4559-E
Jan 2015

Figure 4.11 Net energy metering agreement and customer authorization.

Pacific Gas and Electric Company

APPLICATION
Net Energy Metering Interconnection
For Solar And/Or Wind Electric Generating
Facilities Of 30 Kilowatts Or Less

Part II – Description of the Generating Facilities – Continued

B.4 Photovoltaic Generator 1:

Inverter Manufacturer	Model Number	Nameplate Rating kW/unit	CEC[A] Rating kW/unit	Output Voltage	1 or 3 Phase	Qty
Solar Edge	SE6000A-US	6.000	0.9750	240	1	1

PV Panel Manufacturer	Model Number	Nameplate Rating kW/unit	PTC[B] Rating kW/unit	Total Nameplate Capacity kW		Qty
Boviet	BVM6610P-250	0.250	0.2500	6.000		24
				0.000		

B.4 Photovoltaic Generator 2:

Inverter Manufacturer	Model Number	Nameplate Rating kW/unit	CEC Rating kW/unit	Output Voltage	1 or 3 Phase	Qty

PV Panel Manufacturer	Model Number	Nameplate Rating kW/unit	PTC Rating kW/unit	Total Nameplate Capacity kW		Qty
				0.000		
				0.000		

C. Wind Turbine Generating Facility Information

☐ Check this box if the inverter is incorporated in the wind turbine. Then complete the Wind Turbine information below and identify the following: Output Voltage: _____(volts); Phase Type: ☐ 1   ☐ 3

Inverter Manufacturer	Model Number	Nameplate Rating kW/unit	CEC Rating kW/unit	Output Voltage	1 or 3 Phase	Qty

Wind Turbine Manufacturer	Model Number	Nameplate Rating kW/unit	CEC Rating kW/unit	Total Nameplate Capacity kW		Qty
				0.000		

D. AC Disconnect Switch

☐ Check this box if no A/C Disconnect Switch is applicable. See Part III, Section C for requirements.

AC Disconnect Manufacturer	Model Number	Rating (amps)	Qty
Schneider Electric	QO235CP Two-Pole Circuit B	35	1

If applicable, is/are the AC Disconnect(s) less than 10 ft. of the PG&E electric meter? ☑ Yes   ☐ No

Note: PG&E's Electric and Gas Service Requirements, also known as the "Greenbook" requires the AC Disconnect Switch to be located 10 feet or less from PG&E's electric revenue meter at the point of common coupling or interconnection and easily seen from the panel. If the AC Disconnect Switch is greater than 10 feet or there is more than one AC Disconnect, a variance request must be submitted as outlined in Part II, Section A.

[A] California Energy Commission (CEC) ratings are available at www.consumerenergycenter.org
[B] PTC: PVUSA Test Conditions. PTC ratings are available at www.consumerenergycenter.org

Please complete this agreement in its entirety
Automated Document, Preliminary Statement, Part A.

Page 3 of 5
Form 79-1151B
Advice 4559-E
Jan 2015

Figure 4.12 Net energy metering application form.

Source: Pacific Gas and Electric

APPLICATION
Net Energy Metering Interconnection
For Solar And/Or Wind Electric Generating
Facilities Of 30 Kilowatts Or Less

Pacific Gas and
Electric Company

E. Basic Single-Line Diagram (SLD) for Solar Projects (check one):

☑ I certify that the SLD below and the PV equipment information in Part II accurately represent the Customer's service, the Generating Facility (there are no other Generator Facility(ies) connected to the service, and the project does not require a Variance Request.

Utility Service: (if using the SLD to the right)

Panel Voltage (volts)	Main Breaker (amps)	PV Breaker Size (amps)
350	125	35

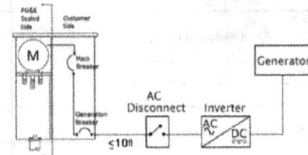

☐ I will submit a custom SLD for one or more of the following reasons: there is/are existing Generating Facility(ies) connected to the service, I am modifying an existing Generating Facility, the Basic SLD does not accurately reflect the project, or I am submitting a Variance Request.
(See Part III Section D for Custom SLD details.)

F. Service Panel Short Circuit Interrupting Rating (SCIR) (for total inverter nameplate ratings larger than 11 kW):

SCIR of the service panel connected to this Generating Facility:_____ watts

Part III – Interconnection Guidelines and Document Information

Note: Applications to interconnect systems located in San Francisco or Oakland may require additional analysis to determine whether or not their proposed installation is on PG&E's networked secondary system. Networked secondary systems are in place to provide heightened levels of reliability in densely populated areas and may affect the ability of PG&E to interconnect NEM customers. Please contact Electric Generation Interconnection department at 415-972-5676 or email gen@pge.com if the proposed installation is in San Francisco where the zip code is 94102, 94103, 94104, 94105, 94107, 94108, 94109, 94111 or 94133 or in Oakland where the zip code is 94607 or 94612.

A. Documents
In addition to this NEM Interconnection Application, the documents listed below are needed to ensure safe and reliable operation of PG&E's Distribution System and to confirm that Customer's interconnection has been performed in accordance with PG&E's tariffs. Additional forms are available on PG&E's website at www.pge.com/standardnem.

Required Documents
- Net Energy Metering (NEM) Interconnection Agreement for Solar and/or Wind Electric Generating Facilities of 30 Kilowatts or Less and Customer Authorization Form 79-1151A.
- Copy of the final, signed, jurisdiction approval (building permit) for Customer's Generating Facility.

Additional Documents (if applicable)
- Variance Request (if project deviates from requirements in Part II Section A).
- Custom Single-Line Diagram (SLD) (if project does not meet Part II Section E basic SLD requirements).

Documents and requirements other than those listed above and/or fees may be required depending on the specifics of the planned Generating Facility.

Please complete this agreement in its entirety
Automated Document, Preliminary Statement, Part A.

Page 4 of 5
Form 79-1151B
Advice 4559-E
Jan 2015

Figure 4.12 (Continued)

In Figure 4.11, the author stated the estimated annual production and usage in kWh to demonstrate net generation. Note, under the PG&E net energy metering (NEM) agreement, NEM systems must be sized *less than 110 percent* of the customer's previous year's kWh usage and account for projected future increases in demand, such as from an extension to the house or an electric vehicle. Essentially, PG&E wants to ensure the residence is not operating as a net energy exporter as the NEM agreement is meant just to offset consumption, or make the customer net zero on consumption. Here we see the customer still has a demand of 7,415 kWh based on the previous years' kWh demand, which is acceptable to PG&E.

A second form, Figure 4.12, was submitted to PG&E that described the array and its components. Most important to PG&E, it identified the AC disconnect was present so the utility knows it can shut off the system in the event of a fault or other issue.

The author submitted the two forms, accompanied by the original approved permitting paperwork, to PG&E, which then performed an inspection of the system at the customer's residence, installed a bidirectional meter, and connected it to the PV inverter.

From the submission of the paperwork to the City of Fairfield to PG&E's approval took approximately three months. The system was interconnected and is now reducing the customer's annual electric bill.

As you can see, the permitting process is highly site-specific and requirements vary by jurisdiction. Current efforts to harmonize permitting requirements across jurisdictions will go a long way toward reducing the soft costs of renewable energy system installations in the U.S. and other developed countries with centralized grids.

Chapter 4 Questions

1. Use the Department of Energy's PVWatts (https://pvwatts.nrel.gov/) to determine if a solar PV array makes economic sense on your or a family member's roof. Use default settings. What is the annual energy (kWh/year) and economic value of your system?

2. Find the climactic data for your region. Using the Exposure C table (Figure 4.6) in the case study, determine the maximum span length of a railing on your roof. Check your local permitting requirements and compare what you have determined against their requirements.

3. Review the "Expedited Permit Process for PV Systems—Standard String System" in the online resources for this book and at http://www.solarabcs.org/about/publications/reports/expedited-permit/forms/index.html. Research online and find PV modules and inverter(s) you would want to use for your house. Using the methods described in Chapter 2, determine your house's electrical consumption per year, the required power output in kW, and the optimal number of modules per string inverter. Draw a sample site plan.

4. Determine the Levelized Cost of Energy (LCOE) of a solar PV system given the following information:
   - PV array of 10 kW
   - $3/watt installed cost
   - 25 year system life
   - 5 peak sun hours and 85 percent efficiency
   - Assume no O&M costs or credits

5. Repeat the calculation in Question 4 with a 30 percent ITC. What is the difference?

6. What is the cost of electricity where you live? Has your PV system reached grid parity? Is it above or below?

7. Review the MREA Small Wind Site Assessment template in the online resources for this book. Determine if your or a family's house would be an ideal location for a small wind turbine.

Chapter 4 Glossary

Asset-backed Security: Cash-flow generating asset, from loans to PPA revenue, packaged together into a tradeable security.

Distributed Energy Resources (DER): Energy source generated close to where it is consumed.

Energy Savings Performance Contract (ESPC): Building owners pay zero upfront for energy efficiency and renewable energy systems. Contractor is paid through resulting energy savings.

Levelized Cost of Energy (LCOE): Method for comparing the value of energy production for diverse energy sources. The total lifetime costs of the asset (design, construction, and operation) divided by the lifetime revenue (income from energy produced).

Non-Utility Generators: Houses, small businesses, and other non-utility entities able to generate electrical power.

Prosumer: an individual or organization that both consumes from the grid and produces energy for the grid.

Public Utility Regulatory Policy Act (PURPA): Legislation passed by the U.S. Congress in 1978 in response to the global energy crisis, with the objective of reducing America's dependence on foreign oil and encouraging renewable energy and energy conservation.

Solar as a Service (SaaS): Users host solar equipment owned and managed by a private company, and pay the company a set price for the resulting energy generated.

Variable Renewable Energy (VRE): Also known as intermittent power source, an energy source where the rate of production cannot be controlled by the generation facility, for example, solar and wind power.

Warehousing: A financing model packaging early-stage renewable energy projects into a single investment vehicle to mitigate risk.

Yieldcos: a high-yield fund made up of renewable energy projects with long-term PPAs.

References

1. Wile, R. April 10, 2014. "The Solar Industry Has Been Waiting 60 Years For This To Happen—And It Finally Just Did." *Business Insider*, http://businessinsider.com/solar-price-terrordome-chart-2014-4 (accessed September 15, 2018).
2. The Economist. November 21, 2012. "Sunny Uplands." https://economist.com/news/2012/11/21/sunny-uplands (accessed September 15, 2018).
3. Brooks, B. July 2012. "Expedited Permit Process for PV Systems." http://solarabcs.org/about/publications/reports/expedited-permit/pdfs/Expermit-process.pdf
4. Zipp, K., and R. Barrett. January 23, 2017. "Solar Financing Trends in 2017." *Solar Power World*, https://solarpowerworldonline.com/2017/01/solar-financing-trends-2017/ (accessed September 15, 2018.)
5. "Renewable Energy Project Warehouse Facilities Are on the Rise | Insights | Skadden, Arps, Slate, Meagher & Flom LLP." Overview|About|Skadden, Arps, Slate, Meagher & Flom LLP, https://skadden.com/insights/publications/2016/01/renewable-energy-project-warehouse-facilities-are(accessed September 15, 2018).

6. Stevenson, D.K. February 07, 2018. "Yieldcos—a Renewable Energy Option for Yield-hungry Investors." *Financial Times*, https://ft.com/content/ca1641fc-0b37-11e8-bacb-2958fde95e5e (accessed September 15, 2018).

7. DNV, GL. 2018. "Securitization of Solar Projects." https://dnvgl.com/cases/securitization-of-solar-projects-86650 (accessed September 15, 2018).

8. Bushong, Steven, Adriana Marcela, Joshua, Nathanael, Samuel, and Mukund. May 23, 2016. "How to Calculate Solar LCOE-and Understand Its Values." *Solar Power World*, https://solarpowerworldonline.com/2016/05/calculate-solar-lcoe-understand-values/ (accessed December 04, 2018).

9. Freeman, J., and J. Simon. 2015. "Analysis of Aurora's Performance Simulation Engine for Three Systems." Technical Paper no.NREL/TP-7A40-64213. *National Renewable Energy Laboratory*. Golden, CO: National Renewable Energy Laboratory.

10. Courtesy of Western Regional Climate Center—Desert Research Institute. (accessed March 1, 2016). Direct link no longer available. Also go to NOAA for US Weather Data. https://www.ncdc.noaa.gov/climate-information.

11. "Structural Criteria for Residential Rooftop Solar Energy Installations." *PV Toolkit Document #5*. City of Fairfield. https://fairfield.ca.gov/civicax/filebank/blobdload.aspx?BlobID=10850

12. "Travis Air Force Base, Fairfield CA Meteorological Data." *NOAA*. ftp://ftp.ncdc.noaa.gov/pub/data/EngineeringWeatherData_CDROM/engwx/travis_ca.pdf

13. Farneth, I. 2018. "New California Setback Rules." July 1st, www.renvu.com. https://www.renvu.com/Learn/New-California-Setback-Rules-July-1st-2018.

14. Included in the online resource for this book.

CHAPTER 5

Model 3: Community-Scale Generation and Microgrids

Community generation and microgrids are becoming an increasingly popular alternative to utilities and distributed energy resources. These systems serve a collection of individual households, businesses or industrial facilities. From the perspective of the utility, they are simpler to manage than individual producers because they aggregate prosumers and reduce points of interconnection. For the customer, grouping individuals compounds purchasing power and provides leverage with generators and the utility.

In addition, combining solar and wind produces more consistent power because they are complementary—wind output is greatest at night and solar production is highest in the middle of the day. Some of the multiple generation sources discussed in Chapter 2 are shown in Figure 5.1, a *hybrid* system, which connects various energy sources and storage for more reliable power for a facility.

Hybrid power systems
Combine multiple sources to deliver non-intermittent electric power

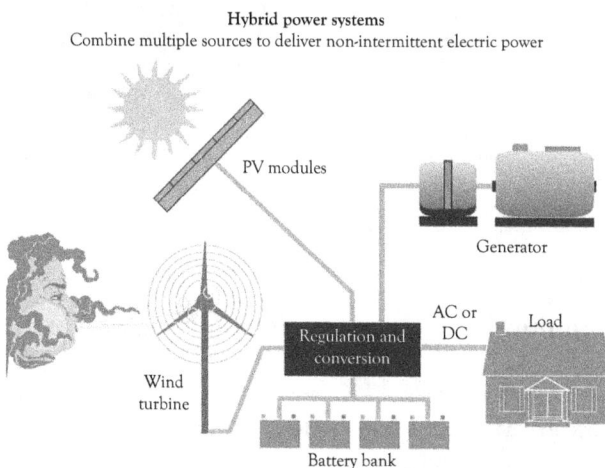

Figure 5.1 Hybrid household power system. Shown above is a residential system with various generators, including a wind turbine, solar PV modules, a generator, and a battery bank for energy storage.
Source: Small Wind Guidebook. US Department of Energy.[1]

Community Generation is a solar, wind, micro-hydro, fuel cell or hybrid energy system whose output is shared by the residents of the immediate area. There are a few ways of implementing such projects. In a *Utility-Sponsored* model, a utility owns and/or operates a system with voluntary participation. With the *Special Purpose Entity* model, individual investors finance the project. In the *Non-Profit* model, community groups fund the project.

Community Generation	
Model	**Sample Program**
Utility-Sponsored	The Sacramento Municipal Utility District (SMUD) contracts with solar developer enXco to offer customers solar energy from a 1 MW PV system. Customers pay a fixed monthly fee based on the amount of PV capacity desired (0.5 to 4 kW) and their average electricity consumption.
Special Purpose Entity	The Clean Energy Collective (CEC) allows for individual membership of a 78 kW PV array in Western Colorado's Holy Cross Energy Service Territory. The CEC leases the land from Holy Cross Energy and has a PPA that will rise with regular utility rate increases. CEC uses a software that directly integrates with the utility's billing system to apply monthly member credits to individuals' accounts.
Non-Profit (Cooperatives)	In Brighton, UK, members of the local community can buy shares in the Brighton Energy Cooperative, a type of cooperative known as a Community Benefit Society. This capital is then used to build solar PV capacity on local rooftops and other prime locations. Until now the business model has been based on feed-in tariffs but the success of cooperatives like the Brighton Energy Cooperative mean that the organization now sells energy on the open market. Rather than directly receiving the energy generated by the co-op, members receive a 5–7 percent return on their investment.[2]

Community Generation Project Development

Similar to the process discussed in Chapter 3, *community generation* projects involve a series of steps. NREL defines the lifecycle of a community project in the following phases: feasibility, project development, construction, operations and maintenance, and decommissioning.[3]

Feasibility	Project development	Construction	Operations and maintenance	Decommiss-ioning

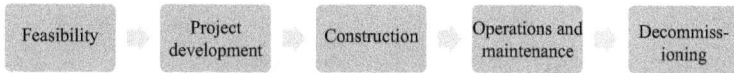

Figure 5.2 Lifecycle of a community generation project as defined by NREL.[4]

In the *feasibility* phase, the team conducts a technical assessment of the solar or wind resource, assesses financing options, and obtains the community's support. During *project development*, the site design and financing are finalized. Also, environmental permits are obtained, the interconnection agreement established, and contractors hired. During *construction*, the architectural and engineering firm and contractor collaborate to realize the design. Often overlooked, *operations and maintenance* involves an ongoing plan for inspections and remote monitoring for verification of performance.

Critical to operations is software that keeps track of members' respective share of the energy. Software as a Service (SaaS) firms have emerged that specialize in managing shared renewable energy assets. Finally, the site must be *decommissioned*, or removed at the end of its life, with consideration to recycling of the spent modules or turbines.

Microgrids

When it comes to a utility figuring out how to manage this wide, dynamic set of resources and control points, the only way they can do that efficiently is to break their networks down into small nodes that is, microgrids—and then add a level of control on top of it.
          —Dave Pacyna, senior vice president of Siemens Energy's
          North American

Microgrids are small, interconnected energy systems that contain a mix of distributed energy resources, storage units and associated loads within a localized grid, forming an island in the central grid. This energy system can operate as part of the wider energy system, but if there is an issue with the wider grid, the microgrid can separate itself and operate independently, ensuring continued energy for its customers.

Comprised of multiple resources, microgrids are more reliable than an individual distributed generator by itself, and provide benefits to the grid, since they can be dispatched to export power to local customers during peak demand conditions. Also, microgrids can alleviate or postpone distribution system upgrades.[5]

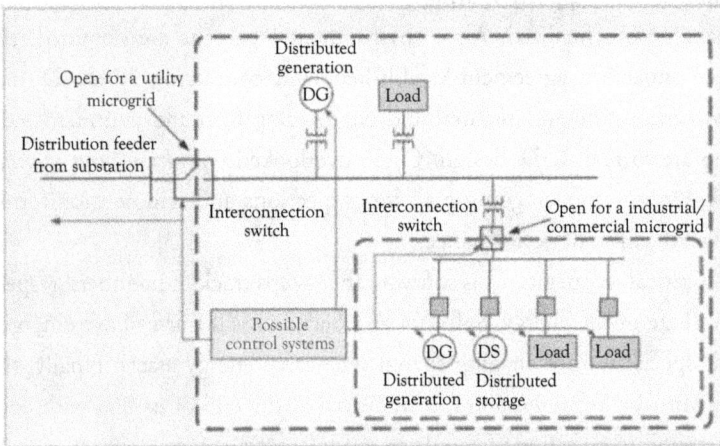

Figure 5.3 Microgrid and its components (electrical loads, distributed generation, distributed energy storage, control systems, and an interconnection switch linking to the central grid).

Source: "Making microgrids work", IEEE Power & Energy Magazine. Kroposki, et al. May-June 2008.[6]

As shown in Figure 5.3, a microgrid consists of several components:

- The *distributed energy resources (DERs)* (aka Distributed Generation-solar, wind, hydro, biomass, and others).
- The *electrical loads* (customers and potential storage).
- A *distribution network* connecting DERs with the loads.
- *Internal sensors and meters* measuring and protecting the microgrid energy supply.
- An *interconnection switch*, or static switch, and a *digital signal processor*, synchronizing power and voltage with the central grid.

- *Computer systems* (often cloud based) for metering, tariffs, and optimization of energy production and demand within the microgrid.

History of Microgrids

In 1998, the U.S. government sponsored the creation of the Consortium for Electricity Reliability Technology Solutions (CERTS), a group of energy stakeholders from the private sector, government research laboratories, and academia. One of the main objectives of CERTS was to find a solution to the issue of long, wide-scale energy blackouts across North America, resulting from extreme weather events, operator errors, and malfunctioning technology within the aging grid.[7] CERTS' research on the problem proposed the "CERTS MicroGrid Concept" as a solution.[8]

CERTS is essentially a protocol for communication between DERs and other components of microgrids. CERTS-compliant products are designed to be versatile in interacting with other components and the grid. For instance, to ensure that the connect-disconnect transition with the wider grid is seamless in the face of grid interruptions, increase the reliability of the islanding mode, and guarantee continued connection for the electrical loads within the microgrid, CERTS does not use a master controller. Rather, they ensure components can operate "peer to peer" so that when an individual component fails, the rest of the system can continue operating. CERTS-compliant systems are also cost-effective since component DERs are compatible with one another via a "plug and play approach" that makes them easily scalable with fewer electronics.

Microgrid Design

Microgrids exist at a range of sizes to ensure energy security for a variety of electrical loads, from a single business, federal facility or laboratory to a residential district.

The amount of the load served by the microgrid defines its purpose. Microgrids covering 30 to 60 percent of loads provide *energy assurance* to critical needs while those covering 100 percent of loads provide *energy independence*. They can even go a step further and provide 100 to 300 percent of the necessary electrical load, *generating revenue*.[9]

The design of a microgrid depends on load requirements, generation mix, components, and its ability to island itself from the wider grid.
A microgrid is highly versatile. Depending on the central grid and DER
production, a microgrid may draw solely from the central grid, a mix of
DERs and the grid, or from the DERs and energy storage alone. This flexibility entails design challenges in terms of the microgrid's energy short
circuit capacity, the need for bi-directional energy flow, and the quality of
the energy generated. The second case study in this chapter explores these
challenges in detail.

Short Circuit Capacity: The central grid uses large, synchronous, rotating power generators, which have a large short-circuit capacity. Standard overcurrent protection is designed with this in mind. In contrast,
renewable generators must be linked, or coupled, to the microgrid via
inverters, which can be damaged by high currents. Thus the inverters
are self-limiting in terms of how much current they can conduct, with
a limit only marginally above the level at which they normally conduct
(roughly 120 percent of inverter-rated current). When a microgrid is in
island mode, the short circuit capacity of the entire system is reduced.
Without adequate planning and system design, this can result in frequent
system interruptions.

Bi-directional energy flow: Unlike a traditional centralized grid system,
where energy flows only one way (from generating power stations to
consumers), the flexible nature of energy production and consumption
patterns in a microgrid requires bidirectional energy flow, including but
not limited to:

- From the central grid to electrical loads within the microgrid
- From the microgrid to microgrid storage and the centralized
  grid, during periods of over-production
- From DERs and storage to microgrid electrical loads while in
  island mode

Power Quality: Power within a centralized grid is produced at a constant
and predictable rate, controlled by the power plant operators. Production

from DERs is less predictable and can lead to fluctuations in available power that cannot be increased to meet surging electrical load. There may be additional fluctuations in harmonics, frequency, transients and voltage. To ensure no damage occurs to the microgrid, its components or electrical loads, these parameters must be monitored and managed to maintain a stable frequency and voltage.

Power Control: Traditional rotating, synchronous power generation is *grid forming*, which means that it naturally assists in the creation and regulation of the voltage and frequency of the power within the grid. Inverter-based DERs tend to be grid-tied, which means that they *feed* energy into the grid, but still rely on synchronous power generation to create and maintain the grid voltage and to stabilize frequency. This causes issues for certain loads in a DER-only microgrid in islanding mode. However, newer DER inverters, called *Inverter-Based Generators (IBGs)*, are able to provide a grid-forming function in an islanded microgrid.[10]

Use of the IBGs allows for the nearly instantaneous switching of voltage, current and frequency between grid-tie and islanded mode. For instance, in Figure 5.4, the Main grid line indicates the steady state voltage from the main grid at 230 volts, while the microgrid line indicates the steady state of the microgrid at just under 215 volts, which would be experienced during the islanded mode. When grid-tie is re-established it takes approximately two seconds, in this study, for the microgrid voltage to synchronize with the central grid.

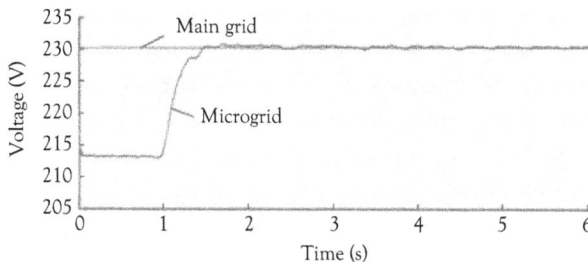

Figure 5.4 Microgrid synchronizing voltage with the central grid during transition from islanded to grid-tie mode.

Source: Papadimitriou, C.N., et al. "Control strategy for seamless transition from islanded to interconnected operation mode of microgrids". Journal of Modern Power Systems and Clean Energy. March 2017.[11]

In addition, IBGs offer other support for the grid, such as supplying reactive power that the grid is accustomed to receiving from conventional generators but is not provided by solar PV systems. Reactive power, which is necessary for motors, can be provided by adjusting the inverter's power factor.

Emerging Trends: Beyond niche projects, stakeholders are beginning to realize the value of community projects and microgrids. With the advent of information communication technologies and monitoring/metering equipment, facilities unable to host their own generators can invest in a microgrid in another location and sell its power and services, such as voltage and frequency support, to the grid through *virtual net metering*. In addition, *fleet microgrids*, or collections of microgrids working in tandem can enable entire communities and potentially cities to become power generators.

Case Study 1: Leapfrogging the Traditional Electrical Grid in Africa Through Microgrids

Richard Driscoll, Former Branch Chief, Office of Global Change, U.S. Department of State

Renewable energy has allowed many in the developing world to "leap-frog," or skip over, the centralized electrical grid. In the last decade, technological and financial innovations brought energy to 130 million people in areas of the world the grid has not yet reached.[12] Africa has been a leader in novel financing options to facilitate access to such systems, from two million users of solar home systems in 2011 to over 53 million in 2016.

East Africa received nearly 60 percent of the total global investment in off-grid solar in 2017. Kenya has been a leader in developing and implementing a form of Solar as a Service known as "pay-as-you-go" (PAYG). AzuriPayGo Energy provides off-grid solar energy to households throughout East Africa. The basic system includes a solar module, inverter, and mobile payment device, and provides sufficient power for lighting, mobile phone charging, and a radio.[13] The consumer pays a small one-time fee for the installation of a solar PV system and then purchases scratch-off cards and uses their mobile phone to top-up their unit. After 18 months, the customer fully owns the system and can use it at no additional charge.

A survey showed that 85 percent of Azuri customers used kerosene lamps prior to installing the solar home system, but only 17 percent used kerosene afterwards. Azuri reports that the solar home system cut weekly energy spending by up to 50 percent. Azuri highlighted the economic benefits in Kitale, Kenya, where one farmer realized a 350 percent increase in her profits because, with lights, she could do her household chores after dark, freeing time in the day to increase her farming production. Similarly, a fishmonger from Kitale has been able to devote additional hours in the marketplace, which has resulted in a 250 percent increase in profits.[14] The potential for replacing fossil fuel with renewable energy off-grid solutions is substantial. IRENA notes that households and small business around the world spend about $36 billion on fossil fuels for lighting, including about $10 billion in Africa alone.

M-KOPA, based in Nairobi, is one of the world's leading "pay-as-you-go" energy providers for off-grid homes. Similar to Azuri, M-KOPA requires an initial deposit of $35, and daily payments of $0.50 for one year until the consumer owns the system.[15] In Mugurameno in Zambia, Standard Microgrid has installed a solar powered microgrid for a community of 32 homes, businesses, and the local primary school.[16]

While the growth of decentralized renewable energy systems in Africa has helped millions, it is posing challenges for policymakers who must develop regulations for interconnection and integration with the national electrical grid.

Case Study 2: Integrating Solar PV and Wind with Diesel Generators

Microgrids combine various generators to provide reliability to a facility or community during a grid outage. The variability of solar and wind requires careful planning and foresight in the design of a microgrid. This is particularly important when the microgrid entails adding wind and solar to existing diesel generators used as backup for a facility.

Many facilities with existing diesel generators are now installing solar or wind energy systems to reduce their CO_2 and other emissions. On one occasion, the author inspected a facility in Burkina Faso, West Africa that had just installed a 380 kW PV system to offset demand from the grid, and from the diesel generator currently used as backup during grid outages. No batteries or energy storage system were installed with the system. In Burkina Faso, blackouts are common, about 6 per day, and last an average of 1.5 hours.

Facility engineers quickly realized that during a grid outage the interaction between the PV system and diesel generator was suboptimal. When the utility power was lost, the PV inverter automatically disconnected due to anti-islanding precautions, and the diesel generator was initiated. Once the PV inverter sensed stable power, the PV system reconnected and supplied power to the facility's loads. However, this caused the generator to fluctuate and operate at as low as 30 percent of its rated load.

Grid-tie PV systems and diesel generators are not designed to share the load. For one, PV inverters shut off during an outage to prevent back-feeding to utility lines. Another critical issue is that PV systems fluctuate based on the sun. This means that diesel generators will be forced to rapidly fluctuate their supply based on the PV output, and operate at low loads. At low loads, typically less than 60 percent of rated load, *wet stacking* occurs in diesel generators. This is a phenomenon in which fuel that is unburned due to the low load ends up in the exhaust pipe. This causes lower cylinder pressures, which lead to poor piston ring sealing and poor combustion. Incomplete combustion causes soot formation and fuel residues that clog the piston rings and pollute the exhaust. Another consequence is glazing, flash burning of the lubricating oil on the cylinder walls.[17] Combined, this increases fuel consumption due to poor efficiency, and degrades the generator, shortening its life.

The simplest solution is an automatic shut-off that prevents the PV array from contributing output while the generator is running, although this would be economically disadvantageous, negating the benefit of the PV supply during outages. Another solution would be to use a natural gas generator, which burns at higher temperatures than diesel engines, and thus would have less unburned fuel while operating at low load. However, it is still not ideal to run a natural gas generator at low load.

Another solution to this problem would be to add energy storage. In systems with diesel generators, solar and battery storage, the batteries could provide consistent power during an outage. As discussed in Chapter 2, in a PV system with battery storage, batteries supply consistent power to either fully or partially cover a facility's loads. Storage provides additional benefits as batteries can supply power at opportune times, when the PV output is low in grid-tie mode, or to partially or completely offset reliance on the backup generator.

Finally, the use of a "hybrid controller" would ensure the diesel generator operates above the minimum load required to maintain acceptable power conversion losses. With such a controller, PV supply is still used to reduce diesel consumption during outages, but limited to maintain the *operating reserve* of the diesel generator. Operating reserve, or spinning reserve, is defined as surplus capacity that allows the diesel generator to handle rapid variability in load or PV supply. It is important to reduce maintenance costs and prolong generator life otherwise subject to frequent start-stop cycles due to the varying PV output.

With a hybrid controller, there are two options during islanded mode. If there is a decrease in load demand, or an increase in PV supply equal to or above demand, the PV inverter is shut off. If there is an increase in load demand, or a decrease in PV output below the diesel generator's minimum, the PV is allowed to contribute to load.

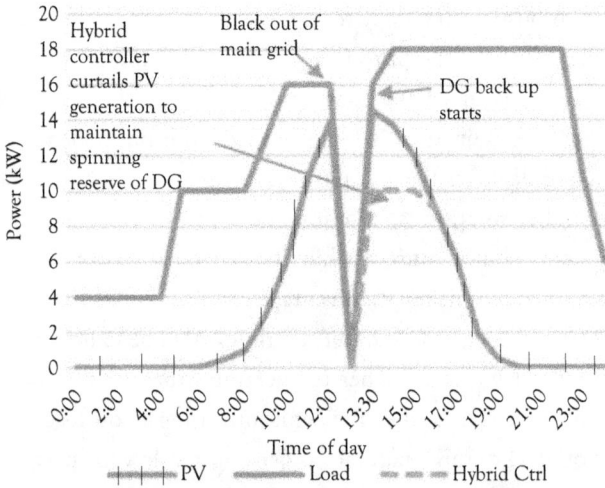

Figure 5.5 *PV curtailment by hybrid controller during grid outage to maintain diesel generator (DG) minimum load. Note the DG production is not shown, but rather the load. PV production is shown at its maximum at noon. In this graph central grid power is lost at 13:30 and PV production is curtailed to allow the DG to run at minimum acceptable load.*[18]

Source: Hybrid Control of Microgrid with PV, Diesel, Generator and BESS. International Journal of Renewable Energy Research.[19]

Thus, in islanded mode, the maximum allowable PV generation is determined by the load minus the minimum diesel generator capacity, as follows:

$$PV_{Max} = \text{Total Load} - \text{Diesel Generator}_{min}$$

Such solutions are commercially available and include, among others, the Fronius PV System Controller.[20]

A Microcosm of the Grid: The interplay/optimization issues between diverse generators explored in this case study are illustrative of the challenges of integrating variable wind and solar energy with conventional "on demand" fossil-fuel generators. As such, the issues with integrating diverse generators in microgrids can be seen as a "microcosm" of the grid at large.

Combined cycle gas turbines (CCGT) are useful for mitigating the intermittency of renewable energy resources. CCGTs are highly efficient because in one cycle they burn natural gas and in the next the exhaust heat generates steam to spin a turbine. CCGTs are able to operate at low loads with high efficiency and few emissions, and can start and stop quickly, a feature known as *fast ramping*.

As more wind and solar comes onto the grid, the flexibility afforded by these generators will become increasingly valuable. Integrating variable renewable energy resources will require diligent foresight, planning, and coordination between developers, utilities and independent system operators. This will ensure the addition of wind and solar does not compromise the security of energy supply, or diminish its economic return. We will discuss grid integration and the shape of a renewable energy dominated future in Chapter 6.

Chapter 5 Questions

1. What are the three models for a community generation project and how do they differ?
2. What is a microgrid and what are its key components?
3. What is the difference between a microgrid and an off-grid renewable energy system?
4. Read the article(s) "Real-World Performance of a CERTS Microgrid in Manhattan" and/or "CERTS Microgrid Demonstration With Large-Scale Energy Storage and Renewable Generation". Note these articles can be found in the endnotes or on the webpage for this book.* Summarize the article(s) in 1 to 2 pages.

---

* Panora, R., J.E. Gehret, M.M. Furse, and R.H. Lasseter. "Real-World Performance of a CERTS Microgrid in Manhattan." *IEEE Transactions on Sustainable Energy* 5, no. 4, 1356–1360. https://ieeexplore.ieee.org/document/6754189
Alegria, E.,T. Brown, E. Minear. and R.H. Lasseter. 2014. "CERTS Microgrid Demonstration with Large-Scale Energy Storage and Renewable Generation." *IEEE Transactions on Smart Grid* 5, no. 2, 937–943. https://ieeexplore.ieee.org/document/6670071

5. Explain the differences and similarities between models of renewable energy development 1, 2 and 3 that have been discussed in Chapters 3 to 5.

6. Do you think a microgrid is needed or would be useful for the area in which you live? Why or why not?

Chapter 5 Glossary

Community Generation: a solar, wind, micro-hydro, fuel cell, or hybrid energy system whose output is shared by the residents of the immediate area.

Inverter-Based Generator (IBG): unlike conventional generators with rotational inertia through the movement of a rotor, solar PV outputs DC at a dissimilar frequency and voltage to the grid. IBGs "clean" the DC output of the PV array and output AC to the grid as a pure sine wave.

Microgrid: a small, interconnected energy system containing a mix of DERs, storage units, and associated loads within a localized grid, forming an island in the central grid.

References

1. Hybrid Wind and Solar Electric Systems. US Department of Energy. "Energy Saver." *Office of Energy Efficiency and Renewable Energy*, https://www.energy.gov/energysaver/buying-and-making-electricity/hybrid-wind-and-solar-electric-systems

2. Brighton Energy Cooperative. 2018. "Community Energy—Invest in Renewables to Support Your Community." https://brightonenergy.org.uk/community-energy-build-community/ (accessed September 16, 2018).

3. NREL. November 2010. "A Guide to Community Solar: Utility, Private and Non-profit Project Development." https://nrel.gov/docs/fy11osti/49930.pdf

4. Id.

5. U.S. Department of Energy. 2018. "How Microgrids Work." https://energy.gov/articles/how-microgrids-work (accessed September 16, 2018).

6. Kroposki, B., R. Lasseter, T. Ise, S. Morozumi, S. Papathanassiou, and N. Hatziargyriou. 2008. "Making Microgrids Work." *IEEE Power and Energy Magazine* 6, no. 3, pp. 40–53.

7. "Microgrids as Risk Mitigation for Extreme Weather." *Electric Light & Power*, March 01, 2013. https://elp.com/articles/print/volume-91/issue-2/sections/microgrids-as-risk-mitigation-for-extreme-weather.html (accessed September 16, 2018)

8. Lasseter, R., A. Akhil, C. Marnay, J. Stephens, J. Dagle, R. Guttromson, A. S. Meliopoulous, R. Yinger, and J. Eto. 2002. "White Paper on Integration of Distributed Energy Resources: The CERTS MicroGrid Concept. Technical paper." *Transmission Reliability Program*. Office of Power Technologies, US Department of Energy.

9. Roach, M. 2014. "Community Power and Fleet Microgrids: Meeting Climate Goals, Enhancing System Resilience, and Stimulating Local Economic Development." *IEEE Electrification Magazine* 2, no. 1, 40–53. doi:10.1109/mele.2013.2297011. https://ieeexplore.ieee.org/document/6774559

10. Boutin, V., V. Ignatova, J. Philippe, R. Heliot, Y. Harriot, A. Haun, and V. Wagner. 2017. "How New Microgrid Technologies Enable Optimal Cooperation Among Distributed Energy Resources." Report no. 998-2095-03-15-17AR0_EN. Schneider Electric. https://schneider-electric.com/en/download/document/998-2095-03-15-17AR0_EN/ (accessed September 16, 2018).

11. Papadimitriou, C.N., V.A. Kleftakis, and N.D. Hatziargyriou. 2017. "Control Strategy for Seamless Transition from Islanded to Interconnected Operation Mode of Microgrids." *Journal of Modern Power Systems and Clean Energy* 5, no. 2, pp. 169–176. https://link.springer.com/article/10.1007/s40565-016-0229-0

12. *Off-Grid Renewable Energy Solutions: Global and Regional Status and Trends*. Report no. ISBN - 978-92-9260-076-1. International Renewable Energy Agency, IRENA. Abu Dhabi, UAE: IRENA, 2018.

13. "AzuriPayGo Energy | Africa." *UNFCCC*, https://unfccc.int/climate-action/momentum-for-change/financing-for-climate-friendly/azuri-paygo-energy (accessed December 04, 2018).

14. Azuri Technologies. June 06, 2017. "Katherine and Suzanne: Housewives, Mothers, Business Women." http://azuri-technologies.com/case-study/katherine-and-suzanne-housewives-mothers-business-women (accessed December 04, 2018).

15. M-KOPA Solar. April 20, 2018. "Battery Technology Energising Off-grid Power Solutions in East Africa." http://m-kopa.com/battery-technology-energising-off-grid-power-solutions-in-east-africa/ (accessed December 04, 2018).

16. "Mugurameno." *Standard Microgrid*, http://standardmicrogrid.com/projects/mugurameno (accessed December 04, 2018).

17. Aurora Generators. May 20, 2016. "What Happens to Engines Running Without Sufficient Loads." https://auroragenerators.com/blogs/generators/119916609-what-happens-to-engines-running-without-sufficient-loads

18. Ganesan, S., V. Ramesh, and S. Umashankar. 2017. "Hybrid Control of Microgrid with PV, Diesel Generator and BESS." *International Journal of Renewable Energy Research (IJRER)* 7, no. 3, pp. 1317–23.

19. Id.

20. "Fronius PV Genset Easy Solution." *Fronius,* https://fronius.com/en/photo-voltaics/products/all-products/solutions/system-solutions/fronius-pv-gen-set-easy-solution/fronius-pv-system-controller

CHAPTER 6

The Emerging Renewable Energy Future

In this book, we have explored the history of electrical systems, learned how various renewable energy technologies work, and discussed models for developing and interconnecting renewable energy projects.

Once a niche market, renewable energy is becoming mainstream, creating new challenges and opportunities. We are living through a fundamental transformation of our electric grid. The successful transition to a predominantly-renewable grid requires the convergence of various forms of innovation, from the *structural* to the *financial* to the *technological*. Well-rounded project managers are needed to implement this shift. Indeed, preparation of future leaders is a key impetus for this book. To conclude our journey, this chapter focuses on the future, exploring the cutting edge of renewable energy integration and technological development.

Challenge 1: Structural

Soft Costs Remain High: As the material costs of solar PV decline rapidly, the industry has encountered an arguably more complex obstacle—disorganization and fragmentation. PV prices for Q4 2018 showed that soft costs (direct labor, engineering and PII, supply chain, overhead, and margin) comprised over half of total installed prices in the commercial sector, and an astounding 65 percent of quoted residential prices.

As shown in Figure 6.1, material prices comprise much less of the system than non-module costs, or *soft costs*. PV system costs have declined rapidly in just the past 20 years, from $5/watt-DC in 1998 to less than $1/watt-DC for utility-scale systems in 2018.

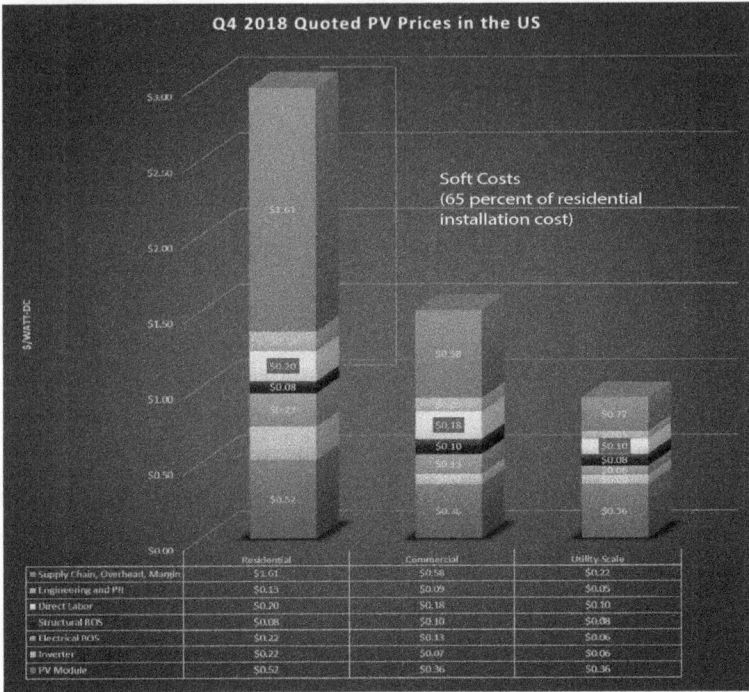

Q4 2018 Quoted PV Prices in the US

Soft Costs
(65 percent of residential
installation cost)

	Residential	Commercial	Utility Scale
Supply Chain, Overhead, Margin	$1.61	$0.58	$0.22
Engineering and PII	$0.13	$0.09	$0.05
Direct Labor	$0.20	$0.18	$0.10
Structural BOS	$0.08	$0.10	$0.08
Electrical BOS	$0.22	$0.13	$0.06
Inverter	$0.22	$0.07	$0.06
PV Module	$0.52	$0.36	$0.36

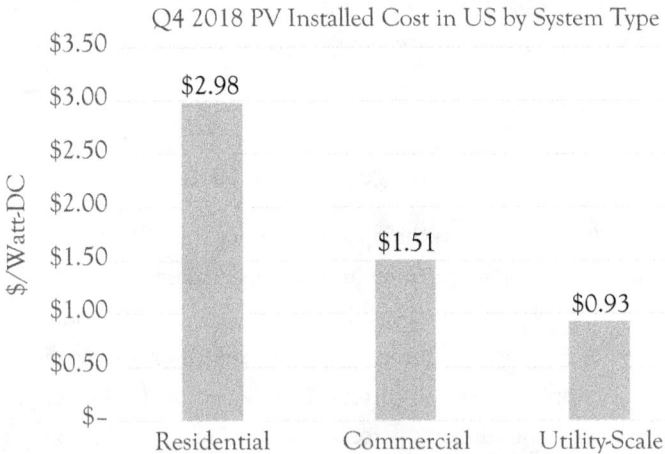

Q4 2018 PV Installed Cost in US by System Type

Figure 6.1 Quoted PV prices in Q4 2018 by system size.
For residential systems, soft costs represented 65 percent of
the total installed cost.

Data from *Wood Mackenzie, Limited/SEIA U.S. Solar Market Insight*

As discussed in Chapter 3, more needs to be done to standardize the permitting process across the thousands of jurisdictions throughout the U.S. More technicians and engineers need to be trained in technology and optimization, and more policymakers and managers need to understand the current landscape to envision and implement effective energy policies.

Overcoming Intermittency: As seen in Chapter 5, variable renewable energy (VRE) creates technical and organizational challenges to existing grids designed for centralized AC generation with readily-dispatchable generators. As more variable solar and wind energy saturates the market, system operators must take actions to mitigate increased fluctuations in supply. Increased penetration of VRE is forcing utilities to invest in new infrastructure and software, which has the effect of reducing the value of that renewable energy.

A concept introduced by the National Renewable Energy Laboratory (NREL), *Economic Carrying Capacity (ECC)*, states that there is a ceiling by which continued VRE deployment as a proportion of aggregate energy supply is no longer economically rational due to variability.[2] Implicit in this concept is that limits to VRE penetration above 30 percent are primarily economic, rather than technical.[2] Determining ECC requires a cost-benefit analysis to work out the economic threshold at which the marginal cost of adding additional renewable energy to the energy mix outweighs the marginal benefit derived from such forms of energy.

Grid Flexibility: To increase the ECC, grids must become more flexible, or rapidly adaptable to changes in the supply and demand for power. There are several ways of improving *grid flexibility*:

- **Grid Forecasting Technologies**—allow system operators to more accurately forecast supply and demand for energy to enable a more efficient use of intermittent renewable energy;
- **Demand Response Technologies**—provide economic incentives to consumers to enable a more predictable and consistent load through moderating the peaks and troughs of energy demand;

- **Grid Infrastructure Technologies**—enable excess energy to be transferred from areas of low demand to high demand or low supply;
- **Fast Ramping Supply Technologies (i.e. Combined Cycle Gas Turbine Plant)**—allow for a rapid supply response in periods of unexpected peak demand; and
- **Energy Storage Technologies**—enable renewable energy to be harvested during periods when supply exceeds demand, and deployed during periods when demand exceeds supply.

Grids can be measured and compared based on their flexibility. Metrics include:[3]

- *Assured Energy Relative to Peak Demand*: this metric examines the ratio of generation from "assured" energy sources relative to peak demand. A common criticism of this metric is that assured capacity is not a proxy for grid flexibility. The energy source, typically the determining factor for "assured energy," is not the only variable that factors into whether a grid is flexible.
- *Max Upward or Downward Change in Supply/Demand that can be met over a Specified Time Horizon*: this metric measures the variability of a grid by examining the peaks and troughs of energy supply/demand and the grid's ability to quickly react to such fluctuations. Where this method is lacking is that it assumes significant data availability and a sufficient number of incidents with measurable data in order to conclude on response time (and cause/effect).
- *Expected "Inflexibility" Incidents over a Specified Time Period*: This method examines the frequency at which supply cannot meet demand. This method relies heavily on simulation. A criticism is that it needs to make wide ranging assumptions on the system operating conditions, which can result in high uncertainty and variability ranges.[3]

A sample framework that allows grid operators to be assessed on relative grid flexibility is the GIVAR III Flexibility Scoring Framework.[4] The framework is a methodology for rating power grid systems based on the ability to accommodate VRE. The result is a pictorial representation of relative grid flexibility based on key parameters. In particular, the framework examines power area size, grid strength, interconnection, number of power markets, and flexibility of the dispatchable generation portfolio. An example of the GIVAR III Flexibility Scoring framework is shown in Figure 6.2. It compares the energy grids of India, Spain and Portugal, Brazil, and Japan.

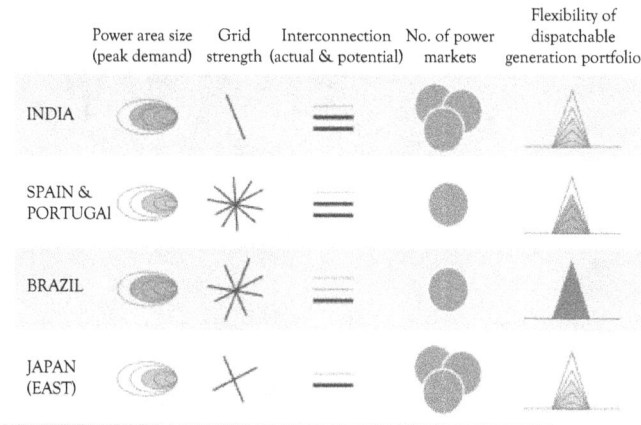

Figure 6.2 *GIVAR III methodology for measuring grid flexibility.*

Source: NREL[5]

A common criticism of GIVAR III is that it does not provide enough information to assess overall flexibility relative to need, or include stochastic or regional changes.[6] Nonetheless, GIVAR III highlights areas where grid flexibility is lacking, which could be a useful roadmap for grid operators to determine where additional investment would reap the greatest improvement.

Valuation: Valuing the excess energy from a grid-tie system has become a contentious issue. Homeowners charged a retail rate for utility electricity expect to be paid the same amount for the energy they provide back to the grid. In *net metering*, a bi-directional meter runs backwards when the homeowner's on-site supply exceeds demand and is exported to the grid. Utilities however, view it differently. For one, as *intermittent power sources*, solar and wind fluctuate during the day with changes in the weather. This means it can be very difficult to match supply with demand.

The "duck curve," developed by the California Independent System Operator (CAISO) demonstrates the challenge of matching demand and supply with increased VRE penetration. The curve shows that non-solar supply must be high in the morning, steeply decline during the "solar window," the three hours before and after 12 p.m. noon, and surge in the afternoon as the sun begins to set.[7]

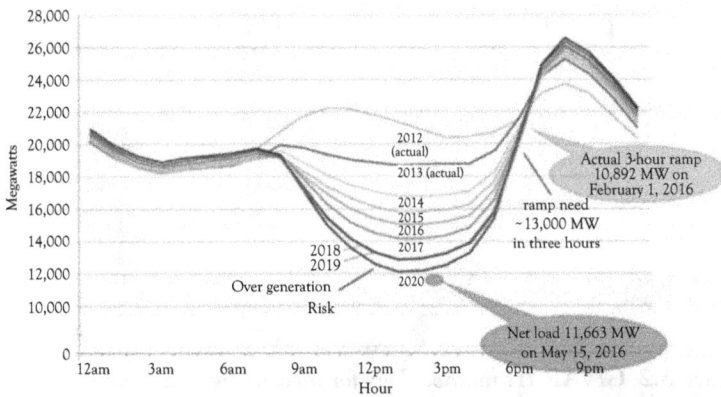

Figure 6.3 The "duck curve"—energy over-generation risk due to peak solar generation at noon when load is lowest on a typical spring day. The curves show net load, which is the difference between forecasted load and expected electricity production from variable renewable energy sources. During the middle of the day, when solar is producing the most energy, net load is low ("belly of the duck"), but then quickly ramps up in the afternoon due to the reduction in solar ("neck of the duck"). As more solar comes on line, the belly will continue to deepen downward.

Source: CAISO[8]

CAISO has taken several steps to better match supply and demand, including *Time of Use (TOU) rates* to deter high use in the evening, and *flexible ramping*, the ability of a generator, typically gas, to vary its output on demand. In the middle of the day, solar resources are the most productive. As discussed in Chapter 1, cycling units provide added flexibility over baseload. They allow a "ramp down" during periods of high solar production, reducing the probability of energy oversupply.

Cycling of power plants causes large thermal losses, a slight increase in emissions, and the potential for mechanical failures, reducing plant life. In October 2016, the Federal Energy Regulatory Commission approved CAISO's "flexible ramping product," which increases the ramp rate, or speed, of power plants to start and stop production. In addition, CAISO pays generators to remain off during high periods of solar production to compensate for lost revenue. As such, CAISO shifts costs to those necessitating flexibility, although currently subsidizes this expense.[9]

Some states have taken a more extreme approach, such as ending net energy metering. Take, for example, Hawaii, which abruptly terminated the program in 2015 after VRE reached 16 percent penetration and Hawaii Electric Industries was unable to manage the intermittent solar energy production.[10]

We are far from consensus on valuating VRE since there are many stakeholders, chiefly utilities, developers, and society at large, each of whom incur costs and benefits from integration. Many *Public Utility Commissions (PUCs)* in the U.S. are conducting *Value of Solar (VoS)* studies to determine the best financial structure both for residential and large-scale interconnections. These VoS studies often take into account the *Triple Bottom Line* approach—considering economic, social, and environmental impacts.

In the following methodology developed for CAISO by Energy and Environmental Economics (E3), the *Net Resource Cost (NRC)*, or total cost of a new renewable energy installation is calculated, taking into account all costs and values to the grid.

NRC, given in $/MWh, is determined by summing all the costs and values from that source.

Net Resource Cost = (Levelized Cost of Energy + Transmission Cost + Integration Cost + Curtailment Cost) – (Capacity Value + Energy Value)

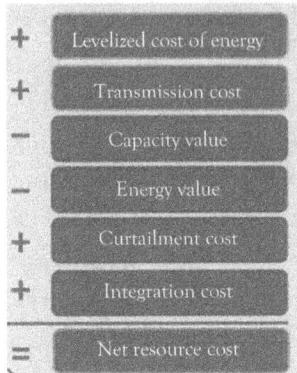

Figure 6.4 Factors comprising net resource cost.

Source: Energy and Environmental Economics, Inc. (E3). RETI 2.0 Plenary Group, Final Plenary Report.[11]

Where:

Table 6.1 Costs and benefits of variable renewable energy

Costs	Benefits
Levelized Cost of Energy (defined on the next page. Also see Chapter 4 for more details.)	**Capacity Value** (the contribution of a power plant to reliably meet demand)
Transmission Cost (new electrical infrastructure and maintenance of existing)	**Energy Value** (the benefit of avoiding fuel costs from natural gas and other fossil fuels).
Integration Cost (electrical interconnection, wholesale energy and capacity costs[12])[13]	
Curtailment Cost (wasted renewable energy when supply exceeds demand)	

Let's look at an example. In a recent analysis, the author evaluated the NRC of solar PV using data from the San Diego Gas and Electric utility. Note that although the original calculation did not incorporate environmental value, the author believes that the health and environmental benefits of avoided non-greenhouse gas emissions from natural gas electric generation should be considered. This is captured in "Environmental Value."

Net Resource Cost = (Levelized Cost of Energy + Transmission Cost + Integration Cost + Curtailment Cost) – (Capacity Value + Energy Value + Environmental Value)

SDG&E's 2016 solar PV supply was 3,453,994 MWh (23 percent of SDG&E's Supply).

2016 SDG&E Net Resource Cost of PV (NRC_{PV}) = ($200,677,051 + $24,177,958 + $111,909,406) − ($51,809,910 + $179,607,688 + $62,171,892)

$$= \$43,174,925$$

Thus, the NRC of solar PV in 2016 was determined to be $43,174,925 for 3,453,994 MWh. This equates to a NRC of $12.50/MWh ($43,174,925/3,453,994 MWh), or $0.01/kWh. Taking only the LCOE and not the NRC, the LCOE would be $58/MWh ($200,677,051/3,453,994 MWh), or $.06/kWh. As you can see, including the energy and environmental value brings the NRC to nearly zero.

$LCOE_{PV}$

This is the Levelized Cost of Energy PV, which is the net present value of PV over its lifetime.

For our calculations, this figure includes capital cost, fixed operations and maintenance, variable operations and maintenance, transmission cost, and the investment tax credit, using a 25 percent capacity factor.

$LCOE_{PV}$ of $58.1/MWh is used[11].
3,453,994 MWh * $58.1/MWh
= $200,677,051

Transmission Cost (included in LCOE)
Often defined as the cost/MW/Mile to accept a new generation source. A levelized cost of $3.8/MWh is used in these calculations and already factored into the above LCOE.

Integration Cost

Commonly referred to as the point of interconnection cost, this includes substation upgrades and power electronics, such as reactive power support and frequency support to harmonize inverter-based generators with the synchronous grid. We use a figure of $7/MWh[1].

$$3,453,994 \text{ MWh} * \$7/\text{MWh}$$
$$= \$24,177,958$$

Curtailment Cost

As illustrated in the CAISO "Duck Curve," curtailment cost represents the amount of excess energy that is wasted when supply exceeds demand. The unsatisfactory quantification of curtailment cost was one of the primary issues in the Southern California Edison Integration Adder Report and reasons for its inconclusive determination. The report used $300/MWh for curtailment and considered it a variable O+M cost[1,1].

Using the optimal 36 percent curtailment rate proposed by Dr. Marc Perez[1,1] and the average wholesale rate of electricity for Southern CA of $90/MWh, the calculations will always fluctuate with the energy production[1,1]

$$3,453,994 \text{ MWh} * \$90/\text{MWh} * 0.36$$
$$= \$111,909,406$$

Capacity Value

Capacity Value refers to the contribution of a power plant to reliably meet demand.[1] For these calculations a CV of $15/MWh is used.[1]

$$3,453,994 \text{ MWh} * \$15/\text{MWh}$$
$$= \$51,809,910$$

Energy Value

Energy Value is closely tied to the price of conventional fuel alternatives, principally natural gas. For these calculations we use an avoided fuel cost of $52/MWh, which reflects natural gas prices from the EIA Annual Energy Outlook 2013 "Reference" case.[1]

$$3,453,994 \text{ MWh} * \$52/\text{MWh}$$
$$= \$179,607,688$$

Environmental Value

Although the original E3 model does not incorporate environmental value, the author believes that the health and environmental benefits of avoided non-greenhouse gas emissions from natural gas electric generation should be integrated. These include sulfur dioxide (SO_2), nitrous oxide (NOX), and particulate matter. We use a figure of $18/MWh[1].

$$3,453,994 \text{ MWh} * \$18/\text{MWh}$$
$$= \$62,171,892$$

As demonstrated, unlike GIVAR III, RETI 2.0 provides a means of comparing aggregate grid flexibility across grids on a relative basis. In addition, the NRC valuation enables the calculation of a "renewable energy adder," or cost for VRE penetration. It is seen as a step forward in terms of its methodology by providing a specific formula rather than a disaggregated pictorial representation, which can only highlight areas where grid flexibility is lacking.

In some studies, the effect of renewable energy adoption on other parameters, such as water supply, are considered. In an analysis for the city of Atlanta, Georgia, the firm Greenlink Group considered the water savings the city would accrue as a result of solar energy consumption, since solar does not require water for cooling as do power plants. The light grey area in Figure 6.5 is the amount of water saved as a result of adoption of solar energy that would have otherwise been put to human use (in million gallons) and the dark grey means water that would have been used and not returned to the watershed, such as for agricultural purposes.

Georgia Water Savings from Solar Adoption in Atlanta

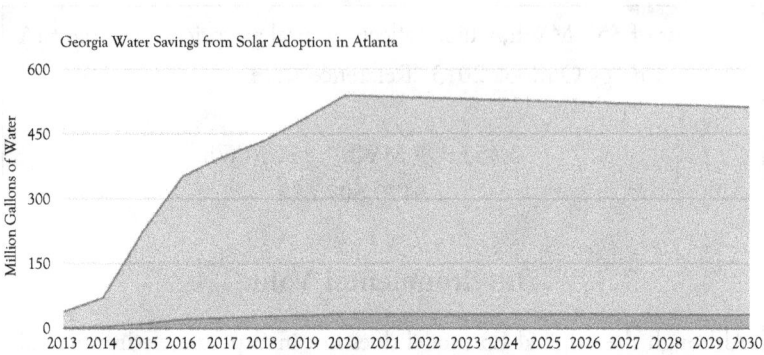

Figure 6.5 Water savings as a result of solar adoption in Atlanta, Georgia are shown in light grey. The smaller dark grey area represents savings of water that would have been used and not returned to the watershed, such as for agricultural purposes.

Source: Greenlink Group, https://www.thegreenlinkgroup.com/

Challenge 2: Financial

The second major challenge is financial. Access to large amounts of capital will be needed to increase solar and wind energy penetration. Unlocking the capital required to reach high penetration of VRE is the frontier of finance in the renewable energy sector.

What's Next in Financing?

The Future of Yieldcos—Master Limited Partnerships (MLPs) inspired the creation of renewable energy yieldcos, discussed in Chapter 4. MLPs are a diversified pool of oil and gas assets that pay no corporate tax and share their revenue with shareholders as dividends. In the U.S., yieldcos spiraled out of control. Yieldcos bought new projects to generate impressive dividends for shareholders, which would boost share prices so that they could buy even more projects. However, when share prices declined, yieldcos still had to pay out promised dividends and could not afford to buy more projects. In the case of SunEdison, this lead to a vicious downward cycle that bankrupted the firm.[14] In the UK, however, solar yieldcos designed for stability offer much more conservative dividends, and are not associated with any one sponsor. American yieldcos are beginning to look much more like their European counterparts.

In the future, the U.S. Congress may broaden its MLP tax benefit to renewable energy projects. Another new mechanism is the Clean Energy Investment Trust (CEIT), a publicly-traded vehicle pioneered by the Rockefeller Foundation. It is distinct from a yieldco in that it is "focused exclusively on yield without the expectations and risks of growth."[15]

Data reducing the cost of debt capital—Granular data enabled by energy measurement, verification and communication technologies are de-risking solar and wind projects, giving investors more confidence. High-quality data collection is opening capital to renewable energy projects. This is particularly important in low-income markets and the developing world, which often have complex ownership models.

Energy storage to capture more value for DERs—As discussed in the structural section, the valuation of renewable energy resources is a hotly-contested issue, necessitating new relationships between utilities and consumers. One exciting area is in using battery storage to increase a system's return on investment. As net metering schemes become less favorable to rooftop solar owners, energy storage systems can provide grid services for which owners will be compensated. For instance, in a recent analysis, Energy Toolbase CEO Adam Gerza showed that SDG&E's new time of use rates reduced the amount PV owners were compensated for during the middle of the day. Energy storage systems that export at times of peak demand and high compensation help to mitigate this erosion of the value of solar.[16]

Challenge 3: Technological

In addition to the structural and financial challenges, increased penetration of VRE will require increasingly efficient and affordable materials. In this section, we will explore a new solar cell technology currently in R&D that shows great promise for commercialization, and the cutting edge of energy storage technologies.

Solar Energy Frontiers

In the mid-20th century, silicon cells were developed at Bell Labs and were very expensive and inefficient. Over the past 60 years scientists have improved Si cell efficiencies, and produced thin films with other materials that are cheaper to produce, yet less efficient. Today, we are working to achieve cheap *and* efficient cells.

In Figure 6.6, the cost and efficiency of the three generations of solar cells are shown. We are currently in the third generation, working toward low cost and high-efficiency cells.

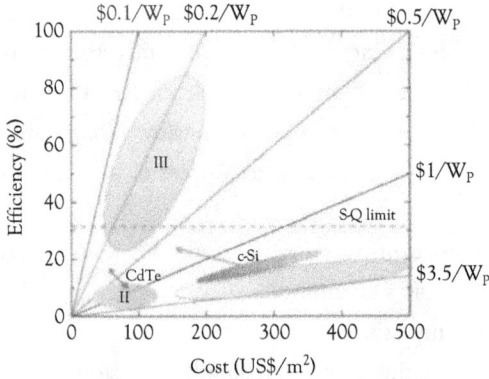

Figure 6.6 Cost and efficiency of three generations of PV cell.

Source: Reproduced from Wolden, C, Kurtkin,J, Baxter, J, Repins, I, Shaheen, S, Torvik, J, Rockett, A, Fthenakis, V, Aydil, E, Photovoltaic Manufacturing: Present Status and Future Prospects, J. Vac. Sci. Technology A29(3) 030801-16, 2011, with the permission of the American Vacuum Society[17]

A member of the third generation, the *Perovskite Solar Cell (PSC)* has been the subject of intense scientific research in recent years due to its rapid rise in efficiency, approaching Silicon's 25 percent photoelectron conversion efficiency, and low manufacturing cost. Although efficiencies have significantly increased in recent years, instability issues impede further development and application. Studies report that volatile species (for example, iodine, I_2) were generated when perovskites were subjected to moisture, oxygen, light illumination, applied electric field, and thermal stress, all of which are relevant to the operation of PSCs in practical applications. They degenerate significantly after 1,000 hours of usage. In addition, there are issues with lead (Pb) toxicity, testing protocols, and ionic movement affecting performance metrics over extended periods of time.[18]

True perovskite minerals are composed of calcium, titanium and oxygen in the form calcium titanate ($CaTiO_3$). Instability and toxicity concerns are currently the focus of research toward commercialization of the cell. PSCs are thermally and chemically unstable compounds that can easily degrade to Pb compounds, which are highly soluble in water. A recent analysis comparing the lead emissions and toxicity potential of lead halide perovskites (LHP–PVs) with that of several existing American utilities, however, revealed that perovskites could actually reduce total lead emissions by a factor of 2 to 4, assuming module efficiency of 17 percent and a lifetime of 20 years.[19]

Further research is needed in several areas to facilitate PSC commercialization. These areas can be characterized as: (1) Optimal perovskite device architecture; (2) Scaling up from lab-scale to production scale; and (3) Environmental, Health, and Safety (EH&S). Areas 1 and 2 include the critical priorities of developing energy-efficient manufacturing processes and improving stability to enable a service life of decades. Area 3 involves assessing the direct risk for consumers as a result of concentrated proximate release of lead, occupational and local population risk assessments, and proper end of life management.

One way in which scientists have leveraged existing manufacturing processes is by sandwiching PSCs with Si, called the *Si-perovskite tandem solar cell*. This cell has high relative stability and efficiency.[20]

Once commercialized, PSCs will dramatically lower costs and could one day be used in the facades, such as windows of buildings themselves.

Energy Storage

Unlike other commodities, electricity cannot be easily stored. Improvements in energy storage technologies, particularly batteries, may have the greatest impact on renewable energy adoption by smoothing variability.

Energy storage does not just include batteries. In fact, utilities primarily use *pumped hydro*, in which the potential energy of water is stored by pumping it up to a reservoir during periods of excess supply, and then reversing the pump during periods of high demand and generating electricity through a turbine.

Figure 6.7 shows various categories of electricity storage technologies categorized by application and timescale.

Categories	Applications	Operation Timescale	Technologies
Power Quality	Frequency Regulation, Voltage Stability	Seconds to Minutes	Flywheels, Capacitors, Superconducting Magnetic Storage, Batteries
Bridging Power	Contingency Reserves, Ramping	Minutes to ~1 Hour	High Energy Density Batteries
Energy Management	Load Following, Transmission/ Distribution Deferral	Hours to Days	Compressed Air Energy Storage, Pumped Hydro, High Energy Batteries

Figure 6.7 Categories of energy storage technologies.

Source: Fthenakis, V., Nikolokakis, T. Comprehensive Renewable Energy. Volume 1, 2012, Pages 199-212. Elsevier. 1.11 – Storage Options for Photovoltaics.[21]

Another analysis of energy storage solutions compares their rated power with their *discharge time*, how long the device outputs electricity. As shown in Figure 6.8, one can clearly see the reason why pumped storage is so widely used by utilities—it has the greatest rated power and discharge time. In addition, pumped storage systems have an expected life of 50 to 60 years.

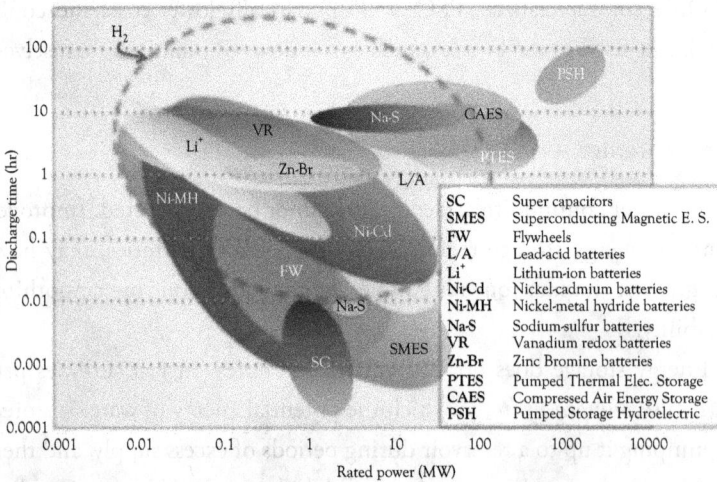

Figure 6.8 Energy storage technologies by rated power and discharge time.[22]

Source: Perez, M. "A Model for Optimizing the Combination of Solar Electricity Generation, Supply Curtailment, Transmission and Storage." Original data from ESA, NREL and DOE/EPRI.[23]

Lithium ion (Li+) has attracted significant interest in the scientific community due to its high energy density, the amount of energy stored in a given volume or mass. However, Li+ must contend with the high supply chain risk of cobalt, which is used for the cathode, the positively-charged electrode in the battery. Most cobalt is found in the Democratic Republic of the Congo where human rights violations and unsafe mining practices abound.

Several firms are commercializing nano-enhanced Li+ energy storage solutions, including A123 Systems' Nanophosphate Li+. In addition to reducing the use of cobalt, nanophosphates increase the cathode surface area with the electrolyte, enabling faster lithium insertion and more power.[24]

Vision for the Future

2020–2030: Jurisdictions worldwide are engaged in a process of valuing renewable energy resources. In the next 10 years, a myriad of location-specific regulations will form with greater complexity than net metering toward an equitable solution for all stakeholders. It will be challenging to apply one solution to all locations, but a standardization will occur once grids increase their flexibility. This process will be enabled by new technologies that allow for greater communication between system components. The rise of the "Internet of Things" (IoT) will hasten the transition to a grid of bidirectional nodes of prosumers, rather than of a central hub with receptive consumers. In preparation for this new reality, protocols for grid-tie inverters, such as California's Rule 21, will provide grid operators with increased confidence in DER synchronization and control.[25]

In addition, the deregulation of the energy sector will grow increasingly sophisticated to permit greater shares of solar and wind in the energy mix. For instance, in October 2018, the city of San Diego, CA with its 1.4 Million people, announced plans to become the largest entity to pursue Community Choice Aggregation, a model that removes the purchase and sale of power from the utility's portfolio, a decision made to hasten the city's goals of 100 percent renewable energy by 2035. Under this plan, by 2021, the utility serving the city, SDG&E, will only be responsible for managing the transmission and distribution lines. Beyond deregulation, the aggregation of multiple customers provides San Diego with the buying power to secure competitive contracts with renewable energy generators.

2030–2050: Greater structural and financial standardization will reduce soft costs. Community generation and microgrids may be the preferred model over DERs as the IoT simplifies communication between individual residents and the grid, and DERs aggregate into larger and fewer nodes for the central utility.

2050s and beyond: Looking more long-term, we can imagine a future unbound by current constraints. In the U.S., wind energy is abundant in states far from urban centers where energy demand is greatest. Imagine if we build transmission lines from wind farms in the midwest states to coastal cities. A 1991 study conducted by the Pacific Northwest Laboratory found that wind turbines in North Dakota could produce 1.2 billion kilowatt-hours of electricity annually—an amount that could supply more than 14,000 times the electricity consumption in the entire state, or 36 percent of 1990 U.S. electricity consumption.

As we have explored, the paramount obstacle to increased solar energy penetration is intermittency. While battery and hydrogen transport and storage costs will decrease, what if we could connect grids across diverse geographical areas to mitigate this intermittency? In a future globally-interconnected grid, solar energy in Asia could power the U.S. at night, and vice versa. Space-based solar power could overcome intermittency by transmitting extra-terrestrial solar radiation through microwave radiation and reflective mirror satellites in geo-synchronous orbit to terrestrial grids.

Concluding Remarks

Renewable energy has come a long way. Over the last decade costs have plummeted, rivaling conventional fuels. Yet serious challenges remain that require engineering and collaboration across disciplines. From integrating solar photovoltaics and wind turbines into the grid at large penetration levels to accessing more sunlight, and converting more of those photons into usable electrons.

We cannot afford to be complacent. In the words of a famous architect of the semiconductor industry, Andy Grove, "success breeds complacency. Complacency breeds failure. Only the paranoid survive."[26]

If we are to transition to a clean energy economy, we need to make renewable energy ubiquitous. For solar cells, while single elements have a maximum efficiency of 31 percent due to the spectrum of light any one material can absorb, research continues into combining multiple materials, concentrating sunlight, and using nanomaterials to achieve greater efficiencies at lower costs. Researchers are developing cells that absorb more high energy photons than silicon with less material and intensive manufacturing, reducing solar's carbon footprint and opening avenues for unforeseen applications.

The past is no guarantee of the future. We are at an inflection point, renewable energy can either peak and stall or continue its rapid climb. Manufacturing improvements have made hydro, wind, solar, and fuel cells viable global energy sources. Now, we must make them our primary ones.

Chapter 6 Questions

1. In your own words, define economic carrying capacity and grid flexibility. Do you think the grid in your country is sufficiently flexible to accommodate variable renewable energy?
2. Do you agree with the net resource calculation done for SDG&E? Do you think there are additional costs or benefits of solar that need to be added? Discuss.
3. What are Perovskite solar cells and why are they receiving a lot of attention in the solar industry?
4. What is your vision for the future of renewable energy and the global energy system?

Chapter 6 Glossary

Flexible Ramping: flexible power generation capacity, able to increase or decrease power output based on real-time demand.

Public Utility Commission: an institution responsible for regulating the energy rates and services of a public utility.

Time of Use (TOU) Rates: scheme whereby the cost of electricity varies based on the time of usage. Energy is most expensive when it is most in demand. Also, under this scheme, on-site systems that export during periods of peak demand are compensated more per kWh than during off-peak.

Triple Bottom Line: "people, planet, profit," an expansion of traditional accounting methodology to incorporate social and environmental costs and benefits.

Value of Solar: a method of quantifying the economic, social, and environmental benefits of solar energy.

References

1. Perea, A., C. Honeyman, S. Kann, A. Mond, M. Shiao, J. Jones, and B. Gallagher. (n.d.). "Solar Market Insight Report 2017 Q2." *GTM & SEIA Research Team*, July 05, 2017. http://seia.org/research-resources/solar-marketinsight-report-2017-q2

2. Cochran, J., P. Denholm, B. Speer, and M. Miller. April, 2015. "Grid Integration and the Carrying Capacity of the U.S. Grid to Incorporate Variable Renewable Energy." November 11, 2017. https://nrel.gov/docs/fy15osti/62607.pdf

3. Cochran, J., M. Miller, O. Zinaman, M. Milligan, D. Arent, B. Palmintier, and B. Kujala. 2014. *Flexibility in 21st Century Power Systems* (No. NREL/TP-6A20-61721). National Renewable Energy Laboratory (NREL). Golden, CO. https://nrel.gov/docs/fy14osti/61721.pdf

4. Id.

5. Id.

6. Id.

7. CAISO. 2016. "What the Duck Curve Tells Us About Managing a Green Grid." https://caiso.com/Documents/FlexibleResourcesHelpRenewables_FastFacts.pdf (accessed August 01, 2017).

8. CAISO. 2016. "What the duck curve tells us about managing a green grid." https://caiso.com/Documents/FlexibleResourcesHelpRenewables_FastFacts.pdf

9. "Fast Ramping: Without it, the Grid's a Sitting Duck." *Enbala Power Networks*, http://cdn2.hubspot.net/hubfs/1537427/NeedforSpeed.pdf?submissionGuid=41eb08c8-555b-49d1-b074-5ded05d82cf9 (accessed August 1, 2017).

10. Customer Renewable Programs. (n.d) "Hawaiian Electric, Maui Electric, Hawaii Electric Light." https://hawaiianelectric.com/clean-energy-hawaii/producing-clean-energy/customer-renewable-programs (accessed October 23, 2018).

11. "E3. RETI 2.0 Plenary Group." *Final Plenary Report*, February 23, 2017. http://docketpublic.energy.ca.gov/PublicDocuments/15-RETI-02/TN216198_20170223T095548_RETI_20_Final_Plenary_Report.pdf

12. There is no standard definition for Integration Cost, although E3 uses language from the California RPS: "expenses resulting from integrating and operating eligible renewable energy resources, including, but not limited to, any additional wholesale energy and capacity costs associated with integrating each eligible renewable resource." http://leginfo.legislature.ca.gov/faces/codes_displaySection.xhtml?lawCode=PUC&sectionNum=399.13

13. "PUBLIC UTILITIES CODE–PUC: DIVISION 1. REGULATION OF PUBLIC UTILITIES [201–3260], PART 1. PUBLIC UTILITIES ACT [201–2120], CHAPTER 2.3. Electrical Restructuring [330–400], ARTICLE 16. California Renewables Portfolio Standard Program [399.11–399.32]." *California Legislative Information*, http://leginfo.legislature.ca.gov/faces/codes_displaySection.xhtml?lawCode=PUC§ionNum=399.13 (accessed December 15, 2018).

14. Hals, T. 2016. "Solar Developer SunEdison in Bankruptcy as Aggressive Growth Plan..." *Reuters*, April 22, 2016. https://reuters.com/article/us-sunedison-inc-bankruptcy-idUSKCN0XI1TC (accessed December 15, 2018).

15. *Innovative Finance: Zero Gap.* Report. The Clean Energy Investment Trust, The Rockerfeller Foundation. https://assets.rockefellerfoundation.org/app/uploads/20170706180708/The-Clean-Energy-Investment-Trust-1.pdf (accessed December 15, 2018).

16. "The Energy Show: Energy Toolbase with Adam Gerza." *SolarWakeup.com*, October 26, 2018. http://solarwakeup.com/2018/10/26/the-energy-show-fuel-cells-are-making-a-comeback/ (accessed December 15, 2018).

17. Wolden, C.A., J. Kurtin, J.B. Baxter, I. Repins, S.E. Shaheen, J.T. Torvik, and E.S. Aydil. 2011. "Photovoltaic Manufacturing: Present Status, Future Prospects, and Research Needs." *Journal of Vacuum Science & Technology A: Vacuum, Surfaces, and Films* 29, no. 3, 030801–16. https://doi.org/10.1116/1.3569757

18. Green, M.A., A. Ho-Baillie, and H.J. Snaith. 2014. "The Emergence of Perovskite Solar Cells." *Nature Photonics* 8, no. 7, pp. 506–14.

19. Billen, P., E. Leccisi, S. Dastidar, S. Li, L. Lobaton, S. Spatari, and J.B. Baxter. 2019. "Comparative Evaluation of Lead Emissions and Toxicity Potential in the Life Cycle of Lead Halide Perovskite Photovoltaics." *Energy* 166, pp. 1089–96.

20. Peplow, M. 2018. "Perovskite Progress Pushes Tandem Solar Cells Closer to Market." *Chemical & Engineering News*, June 11, 2018. https://cen.acs.org/energy/solar-power/Perovskite-progress-pushes-tandem-solar/96/i24 (accessed October 23, 2018).

21. Fthenakis, V.M., and T. Nikolakakis. 2012. *Comprehensive Renewable Energy* 1, pp. 199–212. Elsevier. 1.11 – Storage Options for Photovoltaics. https://sciencedirect-com.ezproxy.cul.columbia.edu/science/article/pii/B9780080878720001062?via%3Dihub

22. Perez, M. 2014. "A Model for Optimizing the Combination of Solar Electricity Generation, Supply Curtailment, Transmission and Storage." *Columbia University*, July 7. https://academiccommons.columbia.edu/doi/10.7916/D8445JP4

23. Id.

24. Chung, S.Y., J.T. Bloking, and Y.M. Chiang. 2002. "Electronically Conductive Phospho-olivines as Lithium Storage Electrodes." *Nature News*, September 22, 2002. https://nature.com/articles/nmat732 (accessed December 15, 2018).

25. Brown, G. n.d. "California's New Smart Inverter Requirements: What "Rule 21" Means for Solar Design." November 11, 2018, https://blog.aurorasolar.com/californias-new-smart-inverter-requirements-what-rule-21-means-for-solar-design

26. Grove, A.S., W.J. Baumol, R.E. Litan, and C.J. Schramm. 2007. *Good Capitalism, Bad Capitalism, and the Economics of Growth*, p. 228.

About the Author

Michael Ginsberg is a Doctor of Engineering Science candidate at Columbia University, specializing in solar energy integration into the electrical grid. In his work with the US Department of State, Michael has performed technical analyses of large-scale solar installs on U.S. compounds worldwide, and trained nearly 1,000 engineers and technicians in renewable energy and building systems at U.S. Embassies in West Africa, South America, the Middle East, and Europe. He is a LEED AP O+M, CEM, NABCEP PV Associate, and holds a MS in Sustainability Management from Columbia University.

Index

OTHER TITLES IN OUR INDUSTRY PROFILES COLLECTION

Donald Stengel, California State University, Fresno, Editor

- *A Profile of the Global Airline Industry* by Kent N. Gourdin
- *A Profile of the Steel Industry: Global Reinvention for a New Economy, Second Edition* by Peter Warrian
- *Company and Industry Research: Strategies and Resources* by Hiromi Kubo and Thomas J. Ottaviano
- *A Profile of the Textile Manufacturing Industry* by Erin D. Parrish
- *A Profile of the Health Management Industry: Health Administration for Non-Clinical Professionals* by Velma Lee
- *A Profile of the United States Toy Industry: Serious Fun, Second Edition* by Christopher Byrne
- *A Profile of the Oil and Gas Industry: Resources, Market Forces, Geopolitics, and Technology, Second Edition* by Linda Herkenhoff

Announcing the Business Expert Press Digital Library

Concise e-books business students need for classroom and research

This book can also be purchased in an e-book collection by your library as

- a one-time purchase,
- that is owned forever,
- allows for simultaneous readers,
- has no restrictions on printing, and
- can be downloaded as PDFs from within the library community.

Our digital library collections are a great solution to beat the rising cost of textbooks. E-books can be loaded into their course management systems or onto student's e-book readers.
The **Business Expert Press** digital libraries are very affordable, with no obligation to buy in future years. For more information, please visit **www.businessexpertpress.com/librarians**. To set up a trial in the United States, please email **sales@businessexpertpress.com**.